THE GARDENER'S YEAR

The Gardener's Year

by KAREL ČAPEK

Illustrated by

JOSEF ČAPEK

The University of Wisconsin Press

Published 1984

The University of Wisconsin Press
114 North Murray Street
Madison, Wisconsin 53715

The University of Wisconsin Press, Ltd.
1 Gower Street
London WC1E 6HA, England

The University of Wisconsin Press printings, 1984, 1985

Library of Congress Cataloging in Publication Data
Čapek, Karel, 1890–1938.
The gardener's year.
Translation of: Zahradníkův rok.
Reprint. Originally published: London: George Allen & Unwin, Ltd., 1931.
I. Title.
PG 5038.C3Z213   1984   635.9'0207   84-40203
ISBN 0-299-10020-3
ISBN 0-299-10024-3 (pbk.)

CONTENTS

THE GARDENER'S YEAR

HOW LITTLE GARDENS ARE LAID OUT

THERE are several different ways in which to lay out a little garden; the best way is to get a gardener. The gardener will put up a number of sticks, twigs, and broomsticks, and will assure you that these are maples, hawthorns, lilacs, standard and bush roses, and other natural species; then he will dig the soil, turn it over and pat it again; he will make little paths of rubble, stick here and there into the ground some faded foliage, and declare that these are the perennials; he will sow seeds for the future lawn, which he will call English rye grass and bent grass, fox-tail, dog's-tail, and cat's-tail grass; and then he will depart leaving the garden brown and naked, as it was on the first day of the creation of

7

the world; and he will warn you that every day you should carefully water all this soil of the earth, and when the grass peeps out you must order some gravel for the paths. Very well then.

One would think that watering a little garden is quite a simple thing, especially if one has a hose. It will soon be clear that until it has been tamed a hose is an extraordinarily evasive and dangerous beast, for it contorts itself, it jumps, it wriggles, it makes puddles of water, and dives with delight into the mess it has made; then it goes for the man who is going to use it and coils itself round his legs; you must hold it down with your foot, and then it rears and twists round your waist and neck, and while you are fighting with it as with a cobra, the monster turns up its brass mouth and projects a mighty stream of water through the windows on to the curtains which have been recently hung. You must grasp it firmly, and hold it tight; the beast rears with pain, and begins to spout water, not from the mouth, but from the hydrant and from somewhere in the middle of its body. Three men at least are needed to tame it at first, and they all leave the place of battle splashed to the ears with mud and drenched with water; as to the garden itself, in parts it has changed into greasy pools, while in other places it is cracking with thirst.

HOW LITTLE GARDENS ARE LAID OUT

If you do this every day, in a fortnight weeds will spring up instead of grass. This is one of Nature's mysteries—how from the best grass seed most luxuriant and hairy weeds come up; perhaps weed seed ought to be sown and then a nice lawn would result. In three weeks the lawn is thickly overgrown with thistles and other pests, creeping, or rooted a foot deep in the earth; if you want to pull them out they break off at the root, or they bring up whole lumps of soil with them. It's like this: the more of a nuisance the more they stick to life.

In the meantime, through a mysterious meta-morphosis of matter, the rubble of the paths has changed into the most sticky and greasy clay that you can imagine.

Nevertheless, weeds in the lawn must be rooted out; you are weeding and weeding, and behind your steps the future lawn turns into naked and brown earth as it was on the first day of the creation of the world. Only on one or two spots something like a greenish mould appears, something thin like mist, and scanty, and very like down; that's grass, certainly. You walk round it on tiptoe, and chase away the sparrows; and while you are peering into the earth, on the gooseberry and currant bushes the first little leaves have broken forth, all unawares; Spring is always too quick for you.

Your relation towards things has changed. If it rains you say that it rains on the garden; if the sun shines, it does not shine just anyhow, but it shines on the garden; in the evening you rejoice that the garden will rest.

One day you will open your eyes and the garden will be green, long grass will glisten with dew, and from the tangled tops of the roses swollen and crimson buds will peep forth; and the trees will be old, and their crowns will be dark and heavy and widely spread, with a musty smell in their damp shade. And you will remember no more the slender, naked, brown little garden of those days, the uncertain down of the first grass, the first pinched buds, and all the earthy, poor, and touching beauty of a garden which is being laid out.

Very well, but now you must water and weed, and pick the stones out of the soil.

HOW A MAN BECOMES A GARDENER

ODD as it may appear, a gardener does not grow from seed, shoot, bulb, rhizome, or cutting, but from experience, surroundings, and natural conditions. When I was a little boy I had towards my father's garden a rebellious and even a vindictive attitude, because I was not allowed to tread on the beds and pick the unripe fruit. Just in the same way Adam was not allowed to tread on the beds and pick the fruit from the Tree of Knowledge in the Garden of Eden, because it was not yet ripe; but Adam—just like us children—picked the unripe fruit, and therefore was expelled from the Garden of Eden; since then the fruit of the Tree of Knowledge has always been unripe.

While one is in the prime of youth one thinks that a flower is what one carries in a buttonhole, or presents to a girl; one somehow does not rightly understand that a flower is something which hibernates, which is dug round and manured, watered and transplanted, divided and trimmed, tied up, freed from weeds, and cleaned of seeds, dead leaves, aphis, and mildew; instead of digging the garden one runs after girls, satisfies one's ambition, eats the fruit of life which one has not produced oneself, and, on the whole, behaves destructively. A certain maturity, or let us say paternity, is necessary for a man to become an amateur gardener. Besides, you must have your own garden. Usually you have it laid out by an expert, and you think that you will go and look at it when the day's work is over, and enjoy the flowers, and listen to the chirping of the birds. One day you may plant one little flower with your own hand; I planted a house-leek. Perhaps a bit of soil will get into your body through the quick, or in some other way, and cause blood-poisoning or inflammation. One claw and the whole bird is caught. Another time you may catch it from your neighbours; you see that a campion is flowering in your neighbour's garden, and you say: "By Jove! Why shouldn't it grow in mine as well? I'm blessed if I can't do better than that." From such beginnings the gardener yields more and more to this newly awakened passion, which is nourished by repeated success and spurred on by each new failure; the passion of the collector bursts out in him, driving him to raise everything according to the alphabet from Acaena to Zausch-neria; then a craze for specialization breaks out in him, which makes of a hitherto normal being a rose—dahlia—or some other sort of exalted maniac. Others fall victims to an artistic passion, and continually alter and rearrange their beds, devise colour schemes, move shrubs, and change whatever stands or grows, urged on by a creative discontent. Let no one think that real gardening is a bucolic and meditative occupation. It is an insatiable passion, like everything else to which a man gives his heart.

I will now tell you how to recognize a real gardener. "You must come to see me," he says; "I will show you my garden." Then, when you go just to please him, you will find him with his rump sticking up somewhere among the perennials. "I will come in a moment", he shouts to you over his shoulder. "Just wait till I have planted this rose." "Please don't worry", you say kindly to him. After a while he must have planted it; for he gets up, makes your hand dirty, and beaming with hospitality he says: "Come and have a look; it's a small garden, but—— Wait a moment", and he bends over a bed to weed some tiny grass. "Come along. I will show you Dianthus musalae; it will open your eyes. Great Scott, I forgot to loosen it here!" he says, and begins to poke in the soil. A quarter of an hour later he straightens up again. "Ah," he says, "I wanted to show you that bell flower, Campanula Wilsonae. That is the best campanula which—— Wait a moment, I must tie up this delphinium." After he has tied it up he remembers: "Oh, I see, you have come to see that erodium. A moment," he murmurs, "I must just transplant this aster, it hasn't enough room here." After that you go away on tiptoe, leaving his behind sticking up among the perennials.

And when you meet him again he will say: "You must come to see me; I have one rose in flower, a pernetiana, you have not seen that before. Will you come? Do!"

Very well; we will go and see him as the year passes by.

THE GARDENER'S JANUARY

"EVEN January is not a time for idleness in the garden", say the handbooks on gardening. Certainly not; for in January the gardener

CULTIVATES THE WEATHER

There is something peculiar about the weather; it is never quite right. Weather always shoots over the mark on one side or the other. The temperature never reaches the hundred years' normal; it is either five degrees below or five degrees above. Rainfall is either ten millimetres below the average or twenty millimetres above; if it is not too dry, it is inevitably too wet.

If people who are not concerned with the weather have so many reasons for complaining about it, what should a gardener say! If too little snow falls, he grumbles that it reaches nowhere; if too much, he says that he is afraid that it will break his conifers and hollies. If there is no snow, he complains of pernicious black frosts; if the thaw sets in, he curses the mad winds which come with it, and have the damnable habit of upsetting his brushwood and other coverings in the garden, or perhaps, devil take them! will even break the trees. If the sun dares to shine in January the gardener is on tenterhooks lest the bushes will burst into bud too soon. If it rains, he fears for his little Alpine flowers; if it is dry, he thinks with pain on his rhododendrons and andromedas. And yet it would be so easy to satisfy him. It would be quite nice if from the first of January it were nine-tenths of a degree below zero, one hundred and twenty-seven millimetres of snow (light and, if possible, fresh), rather cloudy, calm, or with mild winds from the West; and all would be well. But nobody minds us gardeners, and nobody asks us what things ought to be. That's why the world is as it is.

The gardener is at his worst when the black frosts set in. Then the earth stiffens and dries to the bone, day after day, and night after night, deeper and deeper; the gardener thinks of roots which freeze in the soil, dead and hard as stone; of twigs chilled to the pith by the dry and icy wind; of the freezing bulbs, into which in autumn the plant packed all that it had. If I knew that it would help, I would wrap my holly in my own coat, and draw my pants over the juniper; I would take off my own shirt for you, Azalea pontica; I would cover you with my hat, Alum Root, and for you, Coreopsis, nothing is left but my socks: be thankful for them.

There are a number of tricks for deceiving the weather and making it change. If, for instance, I decide to put on the warmest clothes I possess, the temperature usually rises. And a thaw also

sets in if some friends arrange to go to the mountains to ski. And also, when somebody writes an article for the paper, in which he describes the frosts, the healthy coloured cheeks, the crowds on the ice, and other such phenomena, the thaw comes

just when this article is being set up in the com-
posing-room, and people read it while outside a
mild rain is falling, and the thermometer points to
forty-six above zero; then, of course, the reader
says that the papers are full of lies and bluff; bother
the newspapers! On the other hand, cursing, com-
plaints, swearing, snuffling, saying "burrr", and
other incantations have no influence on the weather.

In January the best-known plants are the so-called
flowers on the window-panes. To make them
flourish your room must be fuggy with vapour;
if the air is completely dry you will not raise one
poor little needle, not to mention flowers. Then
the window must not shut properly: where the
wind blows into the window, flowers of ice will
grow. They flourish more with poor people than
with the rich, because the windows of the rich
shut better.

Botanically the flowers of ice are distinguished
by the fact that they are not flowers at all, but
merely foliage. This foliage resembles endive,
parsley, and the leaves of celery, as well as different
members of the family of Cynarocephalae, Cardu-
aceae, Dipsaceae, Acanthaceae, Umbelliferae, and
so on; they may be compared with the genera:
Onopordon or cotton thistle, Charlemagne's

thistle, Cirsium, Notabasis, sea holly, globe thistle, woolly-head thistle, teasel, "saffron thistle", bear's

breech, and with other plants with spiny, feathery, toothed, jagged, cut, clipped, or hackled foliage; sometimes they resemble ferns or palm leaves, and at other times the needles of the juniper; but they never have flowers.

Well, then, "even January is not a time for idleness in the garden", as—certainly only for comfort—the handbooks of gardening assert. First, it is possible to cultivate the soil because frost is supposed to make it crumble. Right! on New Year's Day the gardener rushes into the garden to cultivate the soil. He goes for it with the spade; after a prolonged struggle he succeeds in breaking the spade against the soil, which is as hard as corundum. Then he takes the hoe; if he tries hard he breaks the handle! He fetches the pickaxe, and manages at least to hack up a tulip bulb which he planted in autumn. The only method of tilling the soil is with a hammer and chisel, but this is a slow process which soon tires. Perhaps one may loosen the soil with dynamite, but this the gardener usually does not possess. Well, then, leave it alone till the thaw comes.

And look, the thaw is here, and the gardener rushes into the garden to till the soil. After a while he brings home, stuck to his boots, all that has thawed on the surface; nevertheless he looks happy and declares that the earth is opening already. In the meantime nothing is left but "to do some work ready for the coming season". "If you have a dry spot in the cellar, prepare soil for potting by carefully mixing leafmould, compost, well-rotten cow-dung, and a little sand." Splendid! only there is coal and coke in the cellar; these women

take up all the space with their silly household stores. Perhaps in the bedroom there might be room for a nice little heap of humus——

"Use the winter period for repairing the pergola,

arches, or the summer-house." Exactly; only I happen to have no pergola, arches, or summer-house. "Even in January it is possible to lay down a lawn"—if only there were a place for it; perhaps in the hall, or in the loft. "The chief thing is to watch the temperature in the greenhouse." Very well, I should love to, but I have no greenhouse. These handbooks of gardening don't tell you very much.

And then one must wait and wait! O Lord, this January is very long! If only it were February——

"Can anything be done in the garden in February?"

"Certainly, perhaps even in March."

And in the meantime, without the gardener having suspected, or having done anything, crocuses and snowdrops have pricked through the soil.

SEEDS

SOME people say that charcoal should be added, and others deny it; some recommend a dash of yellow sand, because it is supposed to contain iron, while others warn you against it for the very fact that it does contain iron. Others, again, recommend clean river sand, others peat alone, and still others sawdust. In short, the preparation of the soil for seeds is a great mystery and a magic ritual. To it should be added marble dust (but where to get it?), three-year-old cow-dung (here it is not clear whether it should be the dung of a three-year-old cow or a three-year-old heap), a handful from a fresh molehill, clay pounded to dust from old pigskin boots, sand from the Elbe (but not from the Vltava), three-year-old hotbed soil, and perhaps besides the humus from the golden fern and a handful from the grave of a hanged virgin—all that should be well mixed (gardening books do not say whether at the new moon, or full, or on midsummer night); and when you put this mysterious soil into flower-pots (soaked in water, which for three years have been standing in the sun, and on whose bottoms you put pieces of boiled crockery, and a piece of charcoal, against the use of which other authorities, of course, express their opinions)

—when you have done all that, and so obeyed hundreds of prescriptions, principally contradicting each other, you may begin the real business of sowing the seeds.

With regard to seeds—some look like snuff, others like very light blond nits, or like shiny and blackish blood-red fleas without legs; some are flat like seals, others inflated like balls, others thin like needles; they are winged, prickly, downy, naked, and hairy; big like cockroaches, and tiny like specks of dust. I tell you that every kind is different, and each is strange, life is complex. Out of this big plumed monster a low and dry little thistle is supposed to grow, whereas, out of these yellow nits a fat gigantic cotyledon is supposed to come. What am I to do? I simply don't believe it.

Well, have you sown your seeds yet? Have you put the pots into lukewarm water and covered them with glass? Have you shaded the windows against the sun, and shut them, so that a hotbed of a hundred degrees will be produced in your room? Very well then, now the great and feverish activity of every sower begins—that is, waiting. Drenched with sweat, without coat, in his shirt-sleeves, the breathless watcher bends over the pots, and with his eyes he draws up the sprouts which ought to come out.

SEEDS

The first day nothing comes up, and the watcher tosses in his bed at night, unable to await the morning.

The second day, on the mysterious soil, a tuft of mould appears. He rejoices that this is the first sign of life.

The third day something creeps up on a long white leg and grows like mad. He exalts almost aloud that it is here already, and he tends the first seedling like a mother nursing her child.

The fourth day, when the shoot has stretched to an impossible length, the watcher becomes anxious, for it might be a weed. Soon it is evident that the fear was not unreasonable. Always the first thing, long and thin, which grows in a pot is a weed. Obviously it must be some law of Nature.

Well, then, sometimes on the eighth day, or still later, without any warning, in a mysterious, unregulated moment, for nobody ever saw or caught it, the soil is silently forced apart and the first shoot appears. I always thought that a plant grew either from the seed downwards like a root or from the seed upwards like the haulm of a potato. I tell you that it is not like that. Almost any plant grows from under the seed upwards, lifting the seed on its head like a cap. Think if a child should grow carrying its mother on its head.

It is simply a wonder of Nature; and this athletic deed is performed by almost any shoot. It lifts the seed with an always braver thrust, until one day it drops it and throws it away; and now it stands here, naked and fragile, bulky or lean, and has on its top two such ridiculously small leaves, and between these two leaves something will become visible later.

But what I shall not tell you yet, I have not got so far. It is only two tiny leaves on a pale little leg, but it is so strange, it has so many variations, it is different with every plant—— What did I want to say? Oh, I know—nothing; only that life is more complicated than one can imagine.

In February the gardener carries on with the jobs of January, especially in cultivating the weather. For you ought to know that February is a dangerous time, which threatens the gardener with black frosts, sun, damp, drought, and winds; this shortest month, this addle-egg among the months, this aborted, leap, and altogether unreliable month, excels them all with its wily tricks; therefore beware of it. During the day it wheedles the buds out of the bushes, and at night it blisters them; with one

27

hand it cajoles you, and with the other it makes you feel a fool. God only knows why in leap years one day is added, just to that wayward, catarrhal, sly, and stunted month; in leap years one day should be added to the beautiful month of May, so that there would be thirty-two, and all would be well. What have we gardeners done to deserve that?

Another occupation in February is hunting for the first sign of spring. The gardener does not place any confidence in the first cockchafer or butterfly which usually announces the spring in the papers; in the first place, he does not care for cockchafers, and secondly, this first butterfly is usually the last one of the previous year which has forgotten to die. The first signs of spring for which the gardener is looking are less deceitful. These are:

1. *Crocuses*, which prick forth in his lawn like swollen bulky prongs; one day the prong bursts (no one has ever seen it yet) and makes such a brush of beautiful green leaves; and this is the first sign of spring; further

2. *Garden catalogues* which the postman brings. Although the gardener knows them by heart (just as the *Iliad* begins with Μῆνιν ἄειδε, θεά, the catalogues begin with the words: Acaena, Acantho-limon, Acanthus, Achillea, Aconitum, Adenophora, Adonis, and so on, as every gardener knows), yet

he reads them carefully from Acaena to Wahlen-
bergia or Yucca, at war with himself over the
question of re-orders.

3. *Snowdrops* are another messenger of spring;
at first they are light-green points peeping from the
soil; later they cleave into two fat seed leaves, and
that's all. Then they flower sometimes as early as
the beginning of February, and I tell you that no
victorious palm, or tree of knowledge, or laurel
of glory, is more beautiful than this white and
fragile cup on a pale stem waving in the raw
wind.

4. *Neighbours* are also no uncertain sign of
spring. As soon as they bustle out into their gardens
with spades and hoes, shears and bast, tree-washes,
and powders for the soil, an experienced gardener
knows that spring is at hand; he puts on his old
trousers and bustles out into the garden with
spade and hoe, so that his neighbours also know
that spring is coming, and they shout the joyful
news to one another over the hedges.

The soil opens but does not yet produce a
green leaf; still one can take it as it is, as a bare
and waiting soil. At present it is still the time for
manuring and digging, draining and trenching,
lightening and mixing. Then the gardener finds
that his soil is too heavy, too clayey or too sandy,

too sour or too dry; in short, the passion to improve it somehow springs in him. You may be sure that the soil can be improved by a thousand different means; fortunately the gardener has not usually

got them at hand. In towns it is rather difficult to have at home guano, beech leaves, rotten cow-dung, old plaster, old peat, decomposed sods, weathered molehills, wood humus, river sand, moor soil, mud from a pond, soil from heaths, charcoal, wood ashes, ground bones, horn shavings, old liquid manure, horse-dung, lime, sphagnum, decayed pith from stumps, and other nutritious, lightening, and beneficial material, not counting

a good dozen of nitrogenous, potash, phosphatic, and other kinds of manures.

There are times when the gardener wishes to cultivate, turn over, and compound all the noble soils, ingredients, and dungs. Alas! there would be

31

no space left in his garden for flowers. At least,
then, he improves the soil as well as he can; he
hunts about at home for eggshells, burns bones

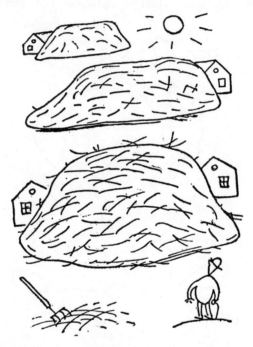

after lunch, collects his nail-cuttings, sweeps soot
from the chimney, takes sand from the sink, scrapes
up in the street beautiful horse-droppings, and all
these he carefully digs into the soil; for all these
are lightening, warm, and nutritious substances.

Everything that exists is either suitable for the soil or it is not. Only cowardly shame prevents the gardener from going into the street to collect what horses have left behind; but whenever he sees on the roadway a nice heap of dung, he sighs at the waste of God's gifts.

When one pictures a mountain of manure in the farmyard—— I know, there are various powders in tin boxes; you can buy whatever you like, all sorts of salts, extracts, slags, and powders; you can inoculate the soil with bacteria; you can till it in a white coat like an assistant at the university or in a chemist's shop. A town gardener can do all that; but when you picture a brown and fat mountain of dung in a farmyard——

But, do you know what? The snowdrops are in flower; and hamamelis with yellow stars is in flower, and hellebore has fat buds; and when you look properly (but you must hold your breath) you will find buds and sprouts on almost everything; with a thousand tiny pulses life rises from the soil. Now we gardeners will stick to it; already we are rushing into sap.

ON THE ART OF GARDENING

WHILE I was only a remote and distracted onlooker of the accomplished work of gardens, I considered gardeners to be beings of a peculiarly poetic and gentle mind, who cultivate perfumes of flowers listening to the birds singing. Now, when I look at the affair more closely, I find that a real gardener is not a man who cultivates flowers; he is a man who cultivates the soil. He is a créature who digs himself into the earth, and leaves the sight of what is on it to us gaping good-for-nothings. He lives buried in the ground. He builds his monument in a heap of compost. If he came into the Garden of Eden he would sniff excitedly and say: "Good Lord, what humus!" I think that he would forget to eat the fruit of the tree of knowledge of good and evil; he would rather look round to see how he could manage to take away from the Lord some barrow-loads of the paradisaic soil. Or he would discover that the tree of knowledge of good and evil has not round it a nice dishlike bed, and he would begin to mess about with the soil, innocent of what is hanging over his head. "Where are you, Adam?" the Lord would say. "In a moment," the gardener would shout over his shoulder; "I am busy now." And he would go on making his little bed.

ON THE ART OF GARDENING

If gardeners had been developing from the beginning of the world by natural selection they would have evolved most probably into some kind of invertebrate. After all, for what purpose has a gardener a back? Apparently only so that he can straighten it at times, and say: "My back does ache!" As for legs, they may be folded in different ways; one may sit on the heels, kneel on the knees,

bring the legs somehow underneath, or finally put them round one's neck; fingers are good pegs for poking holes, palms break clods or divide the mould, while the head serves for holding a pipe; only the back remains an inflexible thing which the gardener tries in vain to bend. The earthworm also is without a back. The gardener usually ends above in his seat; legs and arms are straddled, the head somewhere between the knees, like a grazing mare. He is not a man who would like "to add at least a cubit to his stature"; on the contrary, he folds his stature into half, he squats and shortens himself by all possible means; as you find him he is seldom over one metre high.

Tilling the soil consists, on the one hand, in various diggings, hoeings, turnings, buryings, loosenings, pattings, and smoothings, and on the other in ingredients. No pudding could be more

complicated than the preparation of a garden soil; as far as I have been able to find out, dung, manure, guano, leafmould, sods, humus, sand, straw, lime, kainit, Thomas's powder, baby's powder, saltpetre, horn, phosphates, droppings, cow dung, ashes, peat, compost, water, beer, knocked-out pipes, burnt matches, dead cats, and many other substances are added. All this is continually mixed, stirred in, and flavoured; as I said, the gardener is not a man who smells a rose, but who is persecuted by the idea that "the soil would like some lime", or that it is heavy (as lead the gardener says), and "would like some sand". Gardening becomes a scientific affair. A rose in flower is, so to speak, only for dilettanti; the gardener's pleasure is deeper rooted, right in the womb of the soil. After his death the gardener does not become a butterfly,

intoxicated by the perfumes of flowers, but a garden worm tasting all the dark, nitrogenous, and spicy delights of the soil.

Now in spring gardeners are irresistibly drawn to their gardens; as soon as they lay the spoon down, they are on the beds, presenting their rumps to the splendid azure sky; here they crumble a warm clod between their fingers, there they push nearer the roots a weathered and precious piece of last year's dung, there they pull out a weed, and here they pick up a little stone; now they work up the soil round the strawberries, and in a moment they bend to some young lettuce, nose

close to the earth, fondly tickling a fragile tuft of roots. In this position they enjoy spring, while

over their behinds the sun describes his glorious circuit, the clouds swim, and the birds of heaven mate. Already the cherry buds are opening, young foliage is expanding with sweet tenderness, black-

38

birds sing like mad; then the gardener straightens himself, eases his back, and says thoughtfully: "In autumn I shall manure it thoroughly, and I shall add some sand."

But there is one moment when the gardener rises and straightens himself up to his full height; this is in the afternoon, when he administers the sacrament of water to his little garden. Then he stands, straight and almost noble, directing the jet of water from the mouth of the hydrant; the water rushes in a silver and kissing shower; out of the puffy soil wafts a perfumed breath of moisture, every little leaf is almost wildly green, and sparkles with an appetizing joy, so that a man might eat it. "So, and now it is enough", the gardener whispers happily; he does not mean by "it" the little cherry-tree covered with buds, or the purple currant; he is thinking of the brown soil.

And after the sun has set he sighs with deep content: "I have sweated to-day!"

THE GARDENER'S MARCH

IF we are to describe the gardener's March according to truth and old tradition we must carefully take note of two things: (*a*) what the gardener is supposed and wishes to do, and (*b*) what in fact he does, not being able to do more!

(*a*) Well, he *desires* passionately and with all his might; that is a matter of course: he desires, only to take brushwood away and uncover the flowers, to hoe, manure, trench, dig, turn over, loosen, rake, order, water, multiply, slice, cut, plant, transplant, tie up, sprinkle, dung, weed, sow, clean, clip, chase the sparrows and blackbirds away, smell the soil, poke out shoots with the finger, exult over flowering snowdrops, wipe off sweat, ease his back, eat like a wolf and drink like a fish, go to bed with the spade and get up with the lark, praise the sun and the dew from heaven, feel hard buds, develop the first spring blisters, and altogether live, broadly and vigorously, after the gardener's fashion.

(*b*) Instead, he swears that the soil remains, or is again frozen, he rages at home like a lion imprisoned in a cage when the garden is covered with snow, he nurses his cold by the fire, he ought to go to the dentist, he is summoned to the lawcourts, his aunt, his grandchild, or the devil's grandmother comes to see him, and altogether he loses day after day, persecuted by all possible kinds of bad weather, by blows of destiny, affairs and vicissitudes which accumulate, as if by fate, in the month of March; for beware, "March is the busiest month in the garden, which should be prepared for the coming spring."

Yes, only when he becomes a gardener does a man appreciate those threadbare sayings like "the bitter cold", "the merciless North wind", "the harsh frost", and other such poetic cursings; he even himself uses expressions still more poetic, saying that the cold this year is rotten, damned, devilish, cursed, beastly, and blasted; in contrast to the poets he does not only swear at the North

41

wind, but also at the evil-minded East winds; and he curses the driving sleet less than the feline and insidious black frost. He is partial to pictorial utterances, such as: "the winter resists the assaults of spring", and he feels himself immeasurably humiliated, because in this fight he is powerless to assist in defeating and beating down the

tyrant winter. If only he could attack it with hoe or spade, gun or halberd, he would gird himself and go to fight uttering warlike cries; but he can't do more than wait every evening with his wireless for the latest weather forecast, savagely cursing zones of high pressure over Scandinavia, or deep disturbances over Iceland; for we gardeners know from where the wind blows.

THE GARDENER'S MARCH

For us gardeners the popular saws, too, have convincing validity; we still believe that "Matthias breaks the ice", and if he fails we expect that St. Joseph, the carpenter of heaven, will chop it; we know that "in March we creep behind the stove", and we believe in the three icemen,[1] in the spring equinox, in St. Medard's hood,[2] and other such predictions; from which it is obvious that from the earliest times men have suffered from the weather. No one need wonder if he met with sayings like "on the first of May snow melts on the roof", or that "on St. John of Nepomuk's Day nose and hand may freeze away", or that "on St. Peter and Paul's let us wrap in shawls", that "on St. Cyril and Method's water freezes in the pond", and that "on St. Wenceslas' one winter has passed and another begun"; in short, popular proverbs mostly prophesy unhappy and gloomy things. The existence of gardeners who every year, in spite of these bad experiences with the weather, welcome and unveil the spring is therefore a testimony of the imperishable and miraculous optimism of the human race.

A man who has become a gardener likes to go out of his way to meet people with long memories.

[1] Three saints.
[2] If it rains on St. Medard's Day his hood will drip for forty days.

They are oldish and rather distracted people, who every year say that they do not remember such a spring. If it is cold, they proclaim that they do not remember such a cold spring: "Once, it must be

sixty years ago, it was so warm that violets were in flower on Purification Day." On the other hand, if it is a bit warmer, they assert that they do not remember such a warm spring: "Once, it must be sixty years ago, we went on sledges on St. Joseph's

Day." In short, from the testimonies of those people it is obvious that in point of weather an unbridled waywardness prevails in our climate, and nothing can be done against it.

Yes, nothing can be done; it is the middle of

March, and snow lies on the frozen ground. Lord be merciful to the little flowers of the gardeners.

I will not betray to you how gardeners recognize one another, whether by smell, or some password, or secret sign; but it is a fact that they recognize one another at first sight, whether in the gangways of the theatre, or at a tea, or in a dentist's waiting-room; in the first phrases which they utter they exchange views on the weather ("No, sir, I never remember such a spring"), then they pass to the question of humidity, to dahlias, artificial manures, to a Dutch lily ("damned thing; what's its name, well, never mind, I will give you a bulb"), to strawberries, American catalogues, damage from last winter, to aphis, asters, and other such themes. It is only an illusion that they are two men in dress suits in the gangway of the theatre; in deeper and actual reality they are two gardeners with a spade and a watering-can.

When your watch stops you pull it to pieces and then take it to the watchmaker; if somebody's car stops, he turns up the bottom of his overcoat and sticks his fingers in the machinery, and then sends to the garage. With everything in the world it is possible to do something, but against weather nothing can be done. No zeal, no ambition, no newfangled methods, no meddling or cursing is of any use; the germ opens and a sprout comes up when it is time, and a law has been accomplished. Here you are humbly conscious of the impotence of man; soon you will realize that patience is the mother of wisdom!

After all, nothing can be done.

46

BUDS

To-day, on the 30th of March, at ten o'clock in the morning, the first tiny blossom of forsythia opened. For three days I have been watching its largest bud, a tiny golden pod, so as not to miss this historic moment; it happened while I was looking at the sky to see whether it would rain. To-morrow the twigs of forsythia will be sprinkled all over with golden stars. You simply cannot hold it back. Of course, most of all the lilacs have hurried up; before you notice it, they have made fragile and slender little leaves; you can never watch a lilac. Ribes aureum also opens its ribbed and pleated frills; but the other bushes and trees are still waiting for some imperative "Now!" which will breathe from the earth or from the sky; in that moment all buds will open, and it will be here.

Germination belongs to the phenomena which men call a natural process; it is, however, a real march. Decay is also a natural process, but it does not remind one of a march; I should not like to compose a *tempo di marcia* for the process of decay. But if I were a musician I should compose a "march of buds"; first in a light movement lilac battalions would run and scatter; then the columns of red berries would follow; a heavier formation of apple and pear buds would break in, while the young grass would twang and chirrup on every single string. And to this orchestral accompaniment the regiments of disciplined buds would march, running breathlessly forward "in a splendid formation" as one says of military parades. Left, right; left, right: heavens, what a march!

One says that in spring Nature turns green: it is not quite true, for it also becomes red with pink and crimson buds. There are buds deep scarlet and rosy with cold; others are brown and sticky like resin; others are whitish like the felt on the belly of a rabbit; they are also violet, or blond, or dark like old leather. Out of some pointed lace protrudes; others are like fingers or tongues, and others again like warts. Some swell like flesh, overgrown with down, and plump like puppies; others are laced into a tough and lean prong; others open with puffed and fragile little plumes. I tell you, buds are as strange and varied as leaves and flowers. There will be no end to your discoveries. But you must choose a small piece of earth. If I ran as far as Benešov,[1] I should see less of the spring than if I sat in my little garden. You must stand still; and then you will see open lips and furtive glances, tender fingers, and raised arms,

---

[1] A town about thirty miles from Prague.

the fragility of a baby, and the rebellious outburst of the will to live; and then you will hear the infinite march of buds faintly roaring.

So! While I was writing this, the mysterious "Now!" must have come: the buds which in the morning were still swaddled in tough bands have put forth fragile tips, sprigs of forsythia have begun to shine with golden stars, the swollen pear buds have unrolled a little, and on the points of some other buds gold-green eyes are sparkling. Out of resinous scales young green leaves are shooting, fat buds have burst, and a filigree of ribs and folds is emerging. Don't be shy, blushing little leaf; open, folded little fan; awake, downy sleeper, the order to start has already been given. Strike up fanfares of the unwritten march! Glisten and roll, pipe and sing, you golden brass, drums, flutes, and innumerable violins; for the silent brown and green little garden has set out on its victorious march.

THE GARDENER'S APRIL

APRIL, that is the right and blessed month for the gardener. Let lovers go to Jericho with their praises of May; in May trees and flowers only flower, but in April they bud; this sprouting and shooting, these germs, shoots, and sprouts, are the greatest wonder of Nature, and I shall not tell you one word more about them; sit on your heels and poke with your finger in the puffy soil, holding your breath, for your finger is touching a full and fragile bud. It cannot be described, just as kisses and some few other things cannot be described in words.

But let us return to the frail bud; well, nobody knows how it happens, but it occurs strikingly often that when you step on a bed to pick up some dry twig, or to pull out a dandelion, you usually tread on a shoot of the lily or trollius; it crunches under your foot, and you sicken with horror and shame; and you take yourself for a monster under whose hooves grass will not grow. Or with infinite care you loosen the soil in a bed, with the inevitable result that you chop with the hoe a germinating bulb, or neatly cut off with the spade the sprouts of the anemones; when, horrified, you start back, you crush with your paw a primula in flower, or break the young plume of a delphinium. The more anxiously you work, the more damage you make; only years of practice will teach you the mysteries and bold certainty of a real gardener, who treads at random, and yet tramples on nothing; or if he does, at least he doesn't mind. Well, this is only by the way.

Besides germination April is also the month for planting. With enthusiasm, yes, with wild enthusiasm and impatience you order seedlings from the nurseries, for you cannot exist any longer without them; you promised all your friends who have gardens that you would come for cuttings; I tell you that you are never satisfied with what you already have. And so, one day, some hundred and seventy seedlings meet in your house, and they must be planted immediately; and then you look round in your garden and find with overwhelming certainty that you have no space left for them.

Well, then, in April the gardener is a man who, with a fading plant in his hand, runs round his little garden twenty times looking for an inch of soil where nothing is growing. "No, it's not possible here," he murmurs in a low voice; "here I have those damned chrysanthemums; phlox would smother it here, and here is campion, may the devil take it! Hum, here campanulas have run loose, and near this achillea there is no room either—where shall I put it? Wait a little, here—— No, here is monk's-hood; or here—but here is cinquefoil. It might do here, but it is full of tradescantias; and here—what is it coming up here? I wish I knew. Ha, here is a bit of space; wait, my seedling, in a moment I will make your bed. So, there you are, and now grow in peace."

Yes, but in two days the gardener will discover that he has planted it right on top of the scarlet shoots of the evening primrose.

Gardeners have certainly arisen by culture and not by natural selection. If they had developed naturally they would look differently; they would have legs like beetles, so that they need not sit on their heels, and they would have wings, in the first place for

their beauty, and, secondly, so that they might float over the beds. Those who have had no experience cannot imagine how one's legs are in the way, when there is nothing to stand on; how stupidly long they are if one has to fold them underneath to poke with the finger in the ground; how impossibly short they are if one has to reach to the other side of the bed without treading on a clump of pyrethrum or on the shoots of columbine. If only one could hang in a belt and swim over the beds, or have at least four hands, with only a head and

a cap, and nothing else; or have limbs telescoping like a photographic stand! But because the gardener is outwardly constructed as imperfectly as other people, all he can do is to show of what he is capable: to balance on tiptoe on one foot, to float in the air like a Russian dancer, to straddle four yards wide, to step as lightly as a butterfly or a wagtail, to squeeze into a square inch of ground, to maintain equilibrium against all the laws of gravity, to reach everywhere and avoid everything, and still try to keep some sort of respectability so that people will not laugh at him.

*

Of course, at a passing glance from a distance you don't see anything of the gardener but his rump; everything else, like the head, arms, and legs, is hidden underneath.

Thank you for asking, it's a nice show now: with

all the narcissi, hyacinths, and tazettas; with viola cornuta and omphalodes, saxifrage, draba, and arabis and hutchinsia, and with primroses and spring heather, and with all the flowers which will come to-morrow, or the day after, you will be amazed.

Of course, everyone can wonder. "Oh, this is a nice little purple flower", says a layman, to which the gardener replies slightly offended: "Don't you know that that is Petrocallis pyrenaica?" For the gardener has a great faith in names; a flower

56

without a name, to put it platonically, is a flower without a metaphysical idea; in short, it has not a right and absolute reality. A flower without a name is a weed, a flower with a Latin name is somehow raised to a state of dignity. If a nettle grows on your bed, label it "Urtica dioica", and you will respect it; you will even loosen the soil for it, and manure it with saltpetre. If you are talking with a gardener always ask: "What is the name of this rose?" "This is Burmeester van Tholle," the gardener will tell you happily, "and that one is Madame Claire Mordier"; and he will regard you with respect, thinking that you are a proper and intelligent man. And don't toy with names yourself; don't say, for instance: "Here you have a fine arabis in flower," when the gardener may afterwards thunder upon you: "That? Don't you know that it is Schievereckia Bornmülleri?" It is almost the same, but a name is a name; and we gardeners are particular about good names. For that reason we hate children and blackbirds, because they pull out and mix the labels; and it sometimes happens that we say with astonishment: "Look here, this broom flower is exactly like edelweiss—it is perhaps a local variety; and it certainly is a broom, because it has my label."

. . . No, I don't want to sing the praises of the holiday of labour, but of the holiday of private property instead; and if it doesn't rain, I shall certainly celebrate it by sitting on my heels and saying: "Wait a moment, I will give you a bit of humus, and I will cut this shoot; and you would like to go deeper into the ground, wouldn't you?" And the little alyssum will say "Yes", and I shall put it deeper into the soil. For this is my soil, sprinkled with my own sweat and blood, and that literally; for when one cuts a twig, or a shoot, almost always one cuts a finger, and that also is only a twig or a shoot. A man who has a little garden inevitably becomes a private proprietor; then not any rose grows in it, but his rose; then he does not see, or say, that the cherries are already in flower, but that his cherries are already in bloom. A man who is a proprietor enters into a certain kind of relationship with his neighbours; for instance, as regards the weather, he says, "*We* ought not to have any more rain", or that "*We* have had a nice shower". Besides, he acquires some kind of exclusiveness; he thinks that his neighbour's

[1] The 1st of May in Czechoslovakia is called the Svatek Prace, which means the Labour Day.

trees are brushwood and sticks compared with his own; or he sees that his neighbour's quince would look better in his own garden, and so on. It must be true, then, that private property calls forth certain class and collective interests, in the weather, for instance; but it is equally true that it awakens frightfully strong selfish instincts of private enterprise and property. There is no doubt that a man would go to fight for his faith, but still more willingly and fiercely would he fight for his little garden. The man who is the owner of some yards of land, and is growing something on it, becomes in fact a rather conservative creature, for he is dependent on natural laws a thousand years old; do what you will, no revolution will hasten the time of germination, or allow the lilac to flower before May; so the man becomes wise and submits to laws and customs.

As for you, Campanula Alpina, I will make you a deeper bed. Work! even this messing with the soil you may call work, for I tell you it strains your back and knees; you are not doing this work because work is beautiful, or because it ennobles, or because it is healthy, but you do it so that a campanula will flower and a saxifrage will grow into a cushion. If you wish to celebrate anything, you should not celebrate this work of yours, but the campanula or saxifrage for which you are doing it. And if instead of writing articles and books you stand at a loom or a lathe, you would not do the job because it is work, but because you would get for it bacon and peas, or because you would have a crowd of children, and because you would like to live. And therefore to-day you should celebrate bacon and peas, children, and life, and all that you buy for your work, and that you pay for with your work. Or you should celebrate what "you produce with your work". The roadmenders should not only celebrate their work, but the roads which they have made; on the holiday of labour the weavers should celebrate the miles of ticking and canvas which they have got out of the machines. It is called the holiday of labour and not the holiday of achievement; and yet men should be prouder of what they have done than because they have merely worked.

I asked someone who had visited Tolstoy what the boots were like which Tolstoy had made himself. I was told that they were very bad indeed. If one does a job one ought to do it because one likes it, or because one knows it, or finally because one has to live by it; but to sew boots on principle, work on principle, and for the virtue of it, means to do a job which is not worth much. I should imagine that the holiday of labour would end in glorifying men's cleverness and all the tricks they are up to who know how to take work in the right way. If we celebrated the tricky and clever fellows of all countries the day would turn out unusually merry; it would be a real holiday, the pilgrimage day of life, the holiday of all good fellows.

Well, but this holiday of labour is a serious and earnest day. Never mind little spring phlox, open your first pink chalice.

THE GARDENER'S MAY

Look, for all the bustle of tilling and digging, planting and cutting, we could not talk about the greatest pleasure and special pride of the gardener, his rock or Alpine garden. It is called the Alpine garden probably because this part of the garden gives its owner opportunity for performing hazardous mountaineering feats; if, perhaps, he wants to plant a small androsace between those two stones he must tread with one foot gingerly on this one here, which is a bit shaky, and with the other lightly balance in the air, to avoid crushing a cushion of erysimum or of flowering aubretia;

he must make immense straddles, do knees bend, backward bend, forward bend, lying and standing positions, springs, and lunges, in order to be able to plant, till, poke, and weed among the picturesque and not altogether firm stones of his rock garden.

The cultivation of a rock garden appears in this way as an exciting and elevating sport; besides, it affords you innumerable thrilling surprises when, for instance, at the dizzy height of one yard you discover in the rocks a flowering tuft of the white edelweiss, or of Dianthus glacialis, or of some other so-called child of the highland flora. But what is the use of telling you who have not nursed all those miniature campanulas, saxifrages, campions, speedwells, sandworts, drabas, and iberises, and alyssums, and phloxes (and dryas, and erysimum, and house-leeks, and stonecrops), and lavender, and potentilla, and anemone, and chamomile, and wall cress (and gypsophila, and edraianthus and various thymes), (and Iris pumila, and the Olympic hypericum, and the orange hawkweed, and the rock rose, and gentian, and cerastium, and thrift, and toad-flax), (don't forget, of course, Aster alpinus, the creeping wormwood, erinus, spurge, soapwort, and erodium, and hutchinsia, and paronychia, and thlaspi, and aethionema or snapdragon, antennaria, and other innumerable and most beautiful little flowers, as, for instance, petrocallis, lithospermum, astragalus, and others no less important, like primulas, Alpine violets, and others); well, then, one who has not cultivated all these plants, not counting many others (of which

I must mention onosma, acaena, bahia, and sagina and cherleria), should not talk of the beauties of the world; for he has not seen the most graceful thing which this harsh earth has produced in a moment of tenderness (which lasted only a few thousand years). If only you saw a cushion of Dianthus musalae, covered with the pinkest blossoms that——

But what is the use of telling you? Only the owners of rock gardens know this sectarian rapture.

Yes, for the cultivator of a rock garden is not only a gardener, but a collector as well, and that puts him among the serious maniacs. You need

only show him that your Campanula morettiana has taken root and he will come in the night to steal it, murdering and shooting because he can't live any longer without it; if he is too much of a coward, or too fat to steal it, he will cry and whine to you to give him a tiny cutting. That comes from having bragged and boasted of your treasures before him.

Or it may happen that he sees in a flower-shop a pot without a label, out of which something greenish is pricking forth. "And what have you here?" he bursts out.

"This here?" says the florist, embarrassed, "this is some kind of campanula; I don't know myself which it is——"

"Give it to me", says the maniac, simulating indifference.

"No," says the gardener, "I don't want to sell it."

"Oh, look here," begins the man touchingly, "I have been your customer for such a long time, say, what difference will it make to you?"

After much talking, going and returning to the problematic and nameless pot, making it very clear that he will not go away without it, even if he had to hang about for nine weeks, at last, having made use of all the tricks and dodges of the collector, he takes the mysterious campanula home, chooses for it the best spot in the garden, plants it with infinite tenderness, and comes daily to water and sprinkle it with all the care which this rarity deserves. And the campanula grows like hemp.

"Look," says the proud owner to his guest; "isn't it a queer campanula? Nobody has been able to identify it yet; I am really anxious to see what the flower will be like."

"Is that a campanula?" says the guest. "It has leaves almost like a horse-radish."

"Nonsense! Horse-radish?" retorts the owner. "Horse-radish has much bigger leaves, don't you know, and they are not so glossy. It is a campanula, certainly; but, perhaps", he adds modestly, "it is a new species."

From much watering the campanula grows at an astonishing rate. "Look here," jeers its owner, "you said that it had leaves like a horse-radish. Did you ever see a horse-radish with such big leaves? This, my boy, is some Campanula gigantea; it will have flowers as big as dinner-plates."

At last this unique campanula begins to send up a flowering stem, and on that—"Uhm, it is a horse-radish after all; God knows how it got into that pot in the shop!"

"Tell me," says the guest after some time, "how is that gigantic campanula? Isn't it in flower yet?"

"Oh no, it died. These sensitive and precious kinds, you know—— It must have been some hybrid."

It is always a trouble to get plants. In March the nurseryman usually doesn't send you your order, because it may freeze, and the seedlings are not yet up; in April he does not send them either, because he has too much on hand, and in May because he has generally sold out. "There are no primulas left, but I will send you mullein instead; it has got yellow flowers as well."

But sometimes it happens that the post brings a package of seedlings which you ordered. Hurrah! Right here in this bed I want something very high among monk's-hood and larkspurs; we will certainly put dictamnus there, the plant which is also called dittany or the burning bush; the seedlings which they have sent are rather tiny, but they will grow like wildfire.

A month passes and the seedlings don't grow very much; they look like very short grass—if they were not dictamnus you would say they are dianthus. We must water them properly to make them grow; and look here, they have something like pink flowers.

"Look," says the owner of the garden to an expert visitor; "isn't it a small dictamnus?"

"You mean dianthus", says the guest.

"Of course, dianthus," says the host eagerly; "it was a slip. I was just thinking that among these high perennials a dictamnus would look better, don't you think so?"

Every gardening book will tell you that "it is best to get seedlings from the seed". But they don't say that with seeds Nature has its own special habits. It is a law of Nature that either not one of the seeds will grow, or the whole lot. One says: "Here an ornamental thistle would look very well, say cirsium or onopordon." One buys a packet of each, one sows them, and rejoices how well the seeds come up. Some time later the gardener has to transplant them, and he is happy because he has one hundred and sixty pots with luxuriant seedlings; he says, this raising from seed is still the best thing. And then the time comes when the seedlings ought to be put in the ground; but what can he do with one hundred and sixty thistles? When he has stuck them wherever there is a patch of vacant soil there are still over one hundred and thirty left. What do you mean? He can't throw them into the dustbin when he has raised them so carefully?

"Hi, don't you want a plant of cirsium? It looks very nice, you know!"

"Well, why not?"

Thank Heaven the neighbour has got thirty seedlings with which he runs about distressed, in his garden now, looking where to put them. The neighbours below and opposite still remain—

God help them when they get these ornamental thistles six feet high!

THE BLESSED RAIN

Every one of us must have inherited a bit of a farmer in his blood, even if we have no geraniums or sea-onions growing outside our windows; for when the sun has shone steadily for a week we look anxiously at the sky and say to one another as we meet, "It ought to rain."

"It ought," says the other townee; "I was at Letna the other day and it was so dry that the soil was cracking."

"I went by train to Kolin the other day," says the first; "it was frightfully dry."

"We need a good soaking rain", sighs the other.

"We do, for three days at least", says the first.

But in the meantime the sun scorches, Prague slowly begins to smell of sweating humanity, in the trams people's bodies are dully steaming, men are grumpy and unsociable.

"I think that it will rain", says a sweating creature.

"It ought to", moans the other.

"For a week at least," says the first, "on the grass and crops."

"It is too dry", groans the other.

In the meantime the heat becomes still more oppressive, a heavy pressure develops in the air, storms roll in the sky but do not bring relief to earth and man. But once again storms murmur on the horizon, wind saturated with moisture springs up, and here it is: strings of rain hiss on the pavement, the earth almost breathes aloud, water gurgles, drums, pats, and rattles against the windows, tiptaps with a thousand fingers in the spouts, runs in rivulets, and splashes in puddles, and one would like to scream with joy, one sticks one's head out of the window to cool it in the dew from heaven, one whistles, shouts, and would like to stand barefoot in the yellow streams rushing down the streets. Blessed rain, cooling delight of water. Bathe my soul and wash my heart, glistening and cold dew. I was made evil by the heat, evil and lazy. I was lazy and heavy, dull, material, and selfish. I was parched with drought and suffocated with heaviness and discomfort. Ring, silver kisses with which the thirsty earth receives the patter of the drops; roll on, flying veil of water, washing all. No miracle of the sun can equal the wonder of the blessed rain. Run, troubled water, through the runnels of the earth; water and loosen the thirsty matter which binds us prisoner. We all breathe again, grass, and I, and soil; and all is right with the world.

The hissing downpour stops, as if one pulled

a string; the earth shines with silver vapour, a blackbird shouts in the bush and plays mad pranks; we also want to kick our heels, but instead we go out with bare heads to breathe in the fresh and sparkling humidity of the air and earth.

"It was a marvellous rain", we say to one another.

"Marvellous," we say; "we ought to have more yet."

"We ought," we answer, "but even so it was a blessed little rain."

In half an hour it rains again with long thin threads; that is the real, silent, good rain; quietly and broadly the harvest is raining. It is no more a splashing and hissing torrent; gently falls the aery and quiet shower. Not one drop of you will be wasted, silent dew. But the clouds part, and the sun leans against the thin threads; the threads break, the shower fades away, and the earth breathes with warm humidity.

"That was a regular May shower," we say approvingly, "now everything will be nice and green."

"A few drops more," we say, "and it will be enough."

The sun beats full upon the earth, sizzling heat rises from the damp soil, it is stuffy and foggy, like a hothouse. In one corner of the sky another storm is unrolling; you breathe hot vapour, and a few heavy drops fall to the ground, and from some other land a wind wafts soaked with rainy coolness.

You tire in the damp air as in a lukewarm bath; you breathe drops of dew, you wade in little streams of water, you see white and grey bundles of vapour gathering in the sky; as if the whole world would melt into a soft and warm shower of May.

"It ought to rain a bit more", we say.

THE GARDENER'S JUNE

June is the time for making hay; but as for us, owners of small gardens in towns, please do not think that one dewy morning we shall whet the scythe, and then with open shirt, with powerful rustling sweeps, and singing popular songs, we shall cut the sparkling grass. Things are rather different with us. First of all we want to have an English lawn, green like a billiard cloth, and dense like a carpet, a perfect lawn, a grass-plot without blemish, turf like velvet, a meadow like a table. Well, then, in spring we find that this English lawn consists of bald patches, dandelions, clover, clay, and a few hard and yellow tufts of grass. First it must be weeded; we sit down on our heels and pull out all the mischievous weeds, leaving behind a waste land, trampled, and as bare as if bricklayers or a herd of zebra had been dancing on it. Then it is watered and left to crack in the sun, after which we decide that it really needs cutting.

After having made this decision an inexperienced gardener makes his way to the nearest suburb, and on a bald and dry bank he finds an old woman with a lean goat nibbling twigs or the net of a tennis court.

"Granny," says the gardener in a friendly manner,

"would you like a nice bit of grass for your goat? You can come and cut as much as you like."

"And what will you give me for it?" says the old lady, after some meditation.

"Half a crown", says the gardener, and returns

home to wait for the old woman with the goat and the sickle. But the old lady fails to turn up.

Then he buys a sickle and a whetstone and declares that he need not ask anyone; he will cut the grass himself. But either the sickle is too dull or the urban grass too tough, or something; in short, the sickle does not cut; one must take every stem by the top, stretch it, and hack it at the bottom with the sickle, by which procedure the roots are usually pulled out as well. It goes much quicker with scissors. When at last the gardener has cut, pulled, and wasted his lawn as well as he can, he rakes together a little heap of grass, and he goes and makes his way again to find the old woman with the goat.

"Granny," he says sweetly, "wouldn't you like to have a cock of hay for your goat? It's fine clean hay——"

"And what will you give me for it?" says the old lady after thinking it over.

"One and sixpence", says the gardener, and he runs home to wait for the old woman, who doesn't come to fetch the hay; it is a pity to throw away such nice hay, isn't it?

Finally the dustman takes the hay, but he must get sixpence for it. "You know, sir," he says, "we're not supposed to take it."

A more experienced gardener simply buys a lawn-mower; this is some kind of a thing on wheels; it rattles like a machine-gun, and when one runs it over the lawn, bents are flying about; it is a joy I say. When such a lawn-mower comes into the house all the members of the family, from grandfather to grandson, fight with one another to cut the grass; it is such a joy to rattle about and cut a luxuriant lawn. "Look here," says the gardener, "I will show you how it is done." He then runs over the lawn with the formality of a mechanic and ploughman in one.

"Now let me do it", begs another member of the family.

"Just a bit more", persists the father, claiming his right, and off he goes again rattling and cutting the grass till it flies about. That is the first festal hay harvest.

79

"Listen," says the gardener after some time to another member of the family, "would you like to take the mower and cut the grass? It's a nice job!"

"I know," says the other half-heartedly, "but somehow I have no time to-day."

It is well known that the hay harvest is a time for storms. For some days it is swelling on the earth and in the sky; the sun is scorching and is somehow unpleasant, the ground cracks, and dogs smell; the farmer looks wistfully to the sky, and says that it ought to rain. Sometime later the so-called sinister clouds appear, and a wild wind sets in, driving dust, hats, and torn leaves; then the gardener shoots out into the garden with flying hair, not to defy the elements like a romantic poet, but to tie everything that is shaking in the wind, to take away the tools and chairs, ready to meet the elemental fury. And while in vain he tries to tie up the delphiniums, the first hot drops are

falling; for a moment there is a suffocating calm, and crash! a heavy downpour bursts with rattling thunder. The gardener runs to the doorstep, and with a sinking heart he looks out on his garden lashed by rain and storm; and when it is at its worst, he dashes out to tie up a half-broken lily, like a man who is saving a drowning child. "God Almighty, what a flood!" In the midst of this hailstones fall clattering down, bounce over the ground, and are swept away in streams of dirty water; and in the gardener's heart anxiety for the flowers struggles with a kind of rapture which great elemental phenomena stir in men. Then it rumbles deeper, the flood changes into a cold rain, and thins into a shower. The gardener runs into the cool garden, looks in despair at the lawn covered with sand, on the broken irises, and the battered flower-beds, and while the first blackbird sings again he calls over the hedge to his neighbour: "Hullo, it ought to rain a bit more yet; this is not enough for the trees."

Next day the newspapers describe the catastrophic cloud-burst which has caused terrible damage to the new crops; but they do not say that it has caused heavy damage especially to the lilies, or that it has ruined the Papaver orientale. We gardeners are always neglected.

If it were of any use, every day the gardener would fall on his knees and pray somehow like this: "O Lord, grant that in some way it may rain every day, say from about midnight until three o'clock in the morning, but, you see, it must be gentle and warm so that it can soak in; grant that at the same time it would not rain on campion, alyssum, helianthemum, lavender, and the others which you in your infinite wisdom know are drought-loving plants

—I will write their names on a bit of paper if you like—and grant that the sun may shine the whole day long, but not everywhere (not, for instance, on spiraea, or on gentian, plantain lily,

and rhododendron), and not too much; that there may be plenty of dew and little wind, enough worms, no plant-lice and snails, no mildew, and that once a week thin liquid manure and guano may fall from heaven. Amen." For so it was in the garden of Eden; otherwise things would not have grown in it as well as they did, how could they?

But if I mentioned the words "plant-lice" I should also have added that in June green-fly should be destroyed. For this there are various powders, preparations, tinctures, extracts, infusions, and fumigations, arsenic, tobacco, soft soap, and other poisons, which the gardener tries one after the other, as soon as he notices that on the roses the green and succulent lice have seriously increased. If you use these expedients with a certain care, and in due quantity, you will find that the roses sometimes survive this destruction uninjured, except for the leaves and buds, which look somewhat blasted, while the plant-lice thrive under this treatment so that they cover the twigs like dense embroidery. Afterwards it is possible—with loud expressions of disgust—to squash them on one twig after the other. In this way they are destroyed, but for long afterwards the gardener smells of tobacco extract and grease.

ON MARKET GARDENERS

THERE are certainly some people who, when reading these instructive meditations, will say indignantly: "What! this man here talks of every uneatable root, but he never mentions carrots, cucumbers, kohlrabi or savoys, cabbages, cauliflowers and onions, leeks and radishes, nor celery, chive and parsley, not forgetting a nice head of cabbage! What a gardener is this, when partly out of pride, partly out of ignorance, he omits the most beautiful things that a garden can produce, as, for instance, this bed of lettuce!"

In reply to this charge I say that in one of the numerous phases of my life I also ruled over some beds of carrots and savoys, of lettuce and kohlrabi; I did it certainly out of a feeling of romanticism, wanting to indulge in the illusion of being a farmer. In due time it was obvious that I must crunch every day one hundred and twenty radishes, because nobody else in the house would eat them; the next day I was drowning in savoys, and then the orgies in kohlrabi followed, which were terribly stringy. There were weeks when I was forced to chew lettuce three times a day, to avoid throwing it away. I do not intend to spoil the pleasure of market gardeners by any means; but what they have

grown let them eat. If I were obliged to eat my
roses or nibble the flowers of lilies-of-the-valley,
I think I should lose the respect which I have
towards them.

Besides, we gardeners have already enemies
enough: sparrows and blackbirds, children, snails,
earwigs, and plant-lice; I ask you, should we declare
war on caterpillars? Should we set the white
butterflies against us?

Every citizen dreams sometimes of what he
would do if for one day he became a dictator.
For my part I should order, found, and suppress,
thousands of things on that day; besides others, I
should issue a Raspberry Edict. It would enact
that no gardener, under the penalty of having his
right hand cut off, must plant raspberries near the
hedge. Tell me, what has a gardener done to have
everlasting raspberry suckers from his neighbour's
garden sprouting in the middle of his rhododendrons? These raspberries sprawl underneath the
ground for miles; no hedge, wall, or trench, not
even barbed wire or a warning notice, will stop
them; a raspberry sucker will shoot up in the middle
of a bed of carnations or evening primroses, and
there it is! Every single one of your raspberries
ought to become black with lice! Raspberry suckers
ought to sprout in the middle of your bed. Warts

86

as big as ripe raspberries ought to grow on your face. But if you are a gardener of virtue and rank, you will not plant near your hedges any raspberries, or knot-grass, or sunflower, or other plant which, so to speak, will tread on the private property of your neighbour.

Of course, if you wish to please your neighbour, plant melons along your fence. It once happened to me that from my neighbour's garden, on my side of the fence, a melon grew so huge, so Canaan, so record-breaking, that it caused astonishment to a whole host of publicists, poets, and even of university professors, who could not understand how a fruit so gigantic could have squeezed through the palings of the fence. After some time the melon began to look rather indecent; then we cut it, and ate it for punishment.

THE GARDENER'S JULY

In July, according to the immutable law of gardeners, roses are grafted. It is usually done like this: a briar, a wilding, or stock on which the grafting should be done, is got ready, and then a great amount of bast, and finally a gardening or grafting-knife. When all is ready the gardener tries the blade of the knife on the tip of his thumb; if the grafting-knife is sufficiently sharp it gashes his thumb and leaves an open and bleeding wound. This is wrapped in several yards of lint, from which a bud, rather full and big, develops on the finger. This is called grafting a rose. If a briar is not at hand it is possible to achieve the same result on another occasion, as when making cuttings, pruning side branches or dead flowers, or trimming bushes and suchlike.

After having finished grafting roses the gardener finds that he ought again to loosen the baked and compact soil in the beds. This he does about six times a year, and invariably he throws out of the ground an incredible amount of stones and other rubbish. Apparently stones grow from some kind of seeds or eggs, or continually rise out of the mysterious interior of the earth; or perhaps the earth is sweating these stones somehow. The garden—or cultivated soil, also called humus, or mould—consists mainly of special ingredients, such as earth, manure, leafmould, peat, stones, pieces of glass, mugs, broken dishes, nails, wire, bones, Hussite arrows, silver paper from slabs of chocolate, bricks, old coins, old pipes, plate-glass, tiny

mirrors, old labels, tins, bits of string, buttons, soles, dog droppings, coal, pot-handles, washbasins, dishcloths, bottles, sleepers, milkcans, buckles, horseshoes, jam tins, insulating material, scraps of newspapers, and innumerable other components which the astonished gardener digs up at every stirring of his beds. One day, perhaps, from underneath his tulips he will unearth an American stove, Attila's tomb, or the Sibylline Books; in a cultivated soil anything may be found.

But the main July worry is, of course, the watering and sprinkling of the garden. If the gardener uses watering-cans, he counts the cans like a motorist counts the miles. "Ouf," he announces with the pride of a record-breaker, "to-day I wound up

forty-five buckets." If only you knew what a delight it is when the cold water hisses and splashes on the arid soil; when in the evening it sparkles on flowers and leaves, heavy with the welcome dew; when the whole garden breathes damp and soothed like a thirsty wanderer—"Ahaah", says the wanderer, wiping the foam from his beard. It was a hellish thirst. "Landlord, one more yet." And the gardener runs and fetches one more can for this July drought.

With a hydrant and hose, of course, one can water faster and, so to speak, wholesale; in a relatively short time we have watered not only the beds, but the lawn as well, the neighbour's family at their tea, the passers-by, the inside of the house, all the members of the family, and ourselves most of all. Such a jet from the hydrant has terrific efficacy, almost like a machine-gun; in a jiffy you can drill with it a trench in the earth, mow down the perennials, and wrench crowns from the trees. It refreshes you enormously if you squirt with the nozzle against the wind; it is almost a water cure when it drenches you right through. A hose has also a special predilection for developing a hole somewhere in the middle, where you expect it least; and then you are standing like a god of water in the midst of sparkling jets with a long snake coiled at your feet; it is an overwhelming sight. When you are wet to the skin you contentedly declare that the garden has had enough, and you go to get dry. In the meantime the garden said "Ouf", lapped up your water without a wink, and is as dry and thirsty as it was before.

German philosophers assert that crude reality is simply that which is, whereas the higher and moral order is *das Sein-Sollende*, or which ought to be. Well, then, in July especially the gardener admits this higher order, knowing very well what it *ought* to be. "We need a shower", the gardener says in his characteristic way.

It usually happens like this: when the so-called life-giving rays of the sun drive the temperature above one hundred and twenty; when the grass

turns yellow, leaves wilt, and twigs droop and fade from drought and glare; when the earth cracks and bakes into stone, or crumbles into burning dust, then always—

1. The hose bursts so that the gardener is unable to water.

2. Something happens at the pumping-station, and no water comes, and you are, so to speak, in an oven—a heated and glowing oven.

At such times the gardener waters the soil with his sweat, in vain; just imagine how much he must sweat to have sufficient for a small lawn! Similarly, it is futile to call names, curse, blaspheme, and spit savagely, even if we run into the garden with every expectoration (every drop of water is good!). Then the gardener turns to that higher

order and begins to say fatalistically: "We need a shower."

"And where are you going this year for the summer holidays?"

"I don't mind, but it ought to rain."

"And what do you think of the resignation of Mr. MacDonald?"

"I say that it ought to rain."

"Great Scott! Just think of a beautiful November rain; four, five, six days, the cold, rainy threads

93

are murmuring, it is grey and chilly, and it goes
to the bones——"

As I say, it ought to rain.

Roses, phloxes, helenium and coreopsis, hemero-
callis, gladiolus, campanula, and monk's-hood, and
inula, and dragon's-head, and marguerite—thank

God! flowers enough yet for these bad conditions!
Always something flowers and something is fading;
always you must cut withered stalks, murmuring
(to the flower, not to yourself): "And with you
also it is over."

Look at those flowers, in very truth they are
like women: so beautiful and fresh, you can feast
your eyes on them and never see all their beauty,
always something escapes you, good Lord! when
beauty is so insatiable; but as soon as they begin

94

to fade, I hardly know, but they cease to look after themselves (I am talking of flowers), and if one wished to be brutal, he would say that they look like rags. What a pity, my sweet beauty (I am talking of flowers), what a pity that time is so fleeting; beauty comes to an end, and only the gardener remains.

The gardener's autumn begins in March; with the first faded snowdrop.

A BOTANICAL CHAPTER

As is well known, one can distinguish the glacial flora, the steppe flora, the Arctic, Pontic, Mediterranean, Sub-tropical, marshy, and various others; and that by their origin, or the place where they are found, and where they flourish.

Well, then, if you are interested in plants, you will find that one kind of vegetation flourishes in coffee-houses, and another, shall we say, at pork-butchers; that some kinds and genera grow best at railway-stations, and others in signalmen's boxes; it could be demonstrated, perhaps, by a detailed comparative investigation that another flora flourishes outside the windows of the Catholics, different from that outside the windows of unbelievers and freethinkers: whereas, in fact, in the windows of token shops only artificial flowers thrive, and so on. But because botanical topography is, so to speak, still in swaddling clothes, let us stick to a few clearly distinguished botanical groups.

1. The railway-station flora has two sub-classes: platform vegetation and the station-master's garden. On the platform, usually hanging in baskets, but sometimes also standing on cornices or in the station windows, nasturtiums, lobelias, geraniums,

petunias, and begonias are especially to be found, with dracaenas only at the stations of a higher order. The vegetation of railway-stations is distinguished by an unusually full and richly coloured flowering. The station-master's garden is botanically less characteristic; there you will see roses, forget-me-nots, lobelias, honeysuckle, and other sociologically less differentiated species.

2. The railway flora grows in the signalmen's gardens. It comprises especially althaea, which is also called hollyhock, and sunflower, as well as tropaeolum, rambling roses, dahlias, and sometimes asters; as is well known, these are mostly plants reaching over the hedge, possibly to cheer the passing engine-driver. The wild rail flora grows on railway-banks; it consists particularly of helianthemums, snapdragons, mulleins, chamomiles, bugloss, wild thyme, and other railroad species.

3. The butcher flora grows in butchers' windows, between splayed carcases, hams, lambs, and sausages. It embraces only a few species, especially aucuba, Asparagus Sprengeri, and of cactaceous plants, cereus, and echinopsis; at the pork-butchers' you may also find araucaria, and sometimes primroses in pots.

4. The public-house flora includes two oleanders in front of the gate and aspidistras in the windows;

public-houses specializing in so-called "cottage lunches" have cinerarias in the windows; in restaurants you will see dracaenas, philodendrons, begonias with big leaves, variegated coleuses, lantanas, ficuses, and those plants which the society journalists used to describe with well-turned phrases like "the daïs was submerged under the luscious green of tropical vegetation". In coffee-houses only aspidistras do well, whereas on barrack terraces lobelia, petunia, tradescantia, and even laurel and ivy grow abundantly.

As far as my experience goes no plants will take root at bakers' and gunsmiths', in the stores with cars and agricultural machines, with iron-mongers, furriers, stationers, hatters, and with many other trades. Office windows have either absolutely nothing or red and white geraniums; in general, official vegetation is dependent on the good will and sympathy of the clerk or office chief. Besides a certain tradition obtains here; while in the sphere of railways a rich vegetation is found, nothing whatsoever grows in post and telegraph offices; in a botanical sense self-governing offices are more fertile than Government buildings, among which the offices for inland revenue are a perfect desert. The flora of cemeteries has, of course, a botanical class to itself, and of course there is a festival flora which surrounds the plaster busts of the celebrated; oleander, laurel, palm, and at the very worst, aspidistras belong to it.

As for window flora, there are two kinds: the poor and the rich. That with poor people is usually better; besides, with the rich it dies annually, while they are away for holidays.

In the above survey the botanical abundance of the diverse plant locations is by no means exhausted; I should like sometime to discover what kind of people cultivate fuchsias, and what passion-flowers, or what profession supplies the cactus maniacs, and so on; it may be that there is, or that there will develop, a special communistic flora, or a flora of the Liberal Party. Great are the riches of the world; every craft, nay, more, every political party, could choose its own flora!

THE GARDENER'S AUGUST

AUGUST usually is the time when the amateur gardener forsakes his garden of wonder and goes on leave. The whole year long he vehemently swore that this year he would not go anywhere, that a garden is worth more than all summer resorts, and that he, the gardener, was not such a fool and ass as to be harassed by trains and all the devils; nevertheless, when summer sets in even he deserts the town, either because the nomadic instinct has awakened in him or to keep his neighbours from talking. He departs, however, with a heavy heart, full of fears and cares for his garden; and he will not go until he has found a friend or relation to whom he entrusts his garden for that time.

"Look here," he says, "there is nothing to be done now in the garden in any case; if you come and look once in three days, that will be quite enough, and if something here and there is not in order, you must write me a card, and I will come. So, I am relying on you then? As I said, five minutes will be enough, just a glance round."

Then he leaves, having laid his garden upon the heart of an obliging fellow-creature. Next day the fellow-creature receives a letter: "I forgot to tell you that the garden must be watered every day, the best times for doing it are five in the morning and towards seven in the evening. It is practically nothing, you only fasten the hose to the hydrant and water for a few moments. Will you please water the conifers all over as they stand, and

thoroughly, and the lawn as well? If you see any weeds, pull them out. That's all."

A day after: "It is frightfully dry, will you give every rhododendron about two buckets of tepid water, and each conifer five buckets, and other trees about four buckets? The perennials, which are now in flower, ought to have a good deal of water —write by return post what is in flower. Withered stalks must be cut off! It would be a good thing if you loosened all the beds with a hoe; the soil breathes much better then. If there are plant-lice on the roses, buy tobacco extract, and syringe them with it while the dew is on, or after a rain. Nothing else need be done at present."

The third day: "I forgot to tell you that the lawn must be cut; you can do it easily with the mower, and what the mower does not take, you cut with

clippers. But beware! after mowing the grass it must be well raked, and afterwards *swept with a sweeper*! Otherwise the lawn gets bald patches! And water, plenty of water!"

The fourth day: "If a storm comes, will you please run and look at my garden? A heavy rain sometimes causes damage, and it is good to be on the spot. If mildew appears on the roses, sprinkle them early in the morning while the dew is still

on them with flowers of sulphur. Tie high perennials to sticks so that the wind does not break
them. It is glorious here, mushrooms are growing
and the swimming is beautiful. Don't forget to
water every day the ampelopsis near the house, it
is too dry for it there. Keep for me in a packet the
seeds of Papaver nudicaule. I hope that you have

already mown the lawns. You needn't do anything
else, but destroy earwigs."

The fifth day: "I am sending you a box of
plants, which I dug up here in a wood. They are
various orchids, wild lilies, Pasque flowers, pirolas,
bugworts, anemones, and others. Immediately you
have got the box, open it, and damp the seedlings,
and plant them somewhere in a shady place! Add
peat and leafmould! Plant immediately and water

three times a day! Please cut the side branches of the roses."

The sixth day: "I am sending you by express post a box of plants from the country. . . . They must go into the ground at once. . . . At night you ought to go into the garden with a lamp and destroy snails. It would be good to weed the paths.

I hope that looking after my garden doesn't take up much of your time, and that you are enjoying it."

In the meantime the obliging fellow-creature, conscious of his responsibilities, waters, mows, tills, weeds, and wanders round with the box of seedlings looking where the devil he can plant them; he sweats, and is muddied all over; he notices with horror that here some damned plant is fading, and there some stalks are broken, and that the lawn has become rusty, and that the whole garden is somehow looking blasted, and he curses the moment when he took upon himself this burden, and he prays to Heaven for autumn to come.

And in the meantime the owner of the garden thinks with uneasiness of his flowers and lawns, sleeps badly, curses because the obliging fellow-creature is not sending him reports every day on the state of the garden, and he counts the days to his return, posting every other day a box of plants from the country and a letter with a dozen urgent commands. Finally he returns; still with the baggage in his hands he rushes into his garden and looks round with damp eyes—

"That laggard, that dolt, that pig," he thinks bitterly, "he has made a mess of my garden!"

"Thank you", he says dryly to his fellow-creature, and like a living reproach he snatches the hose to water the neglected garden. (That idiot, he thinks in the bottom of his heart, to trust him with anything! Never in my life will I be such a fool and ass to go away for holidays!)

As for the wild plants, the garden maniac digs them somehow out of the soil, to incorporate them in his garden; it is more difficult with other natural objects. "Damn!" thinks the gardener, looking at the Matterhorn or on the Gerlachovka; "if only I had this mountain in my garden; and this bit of forest with its enormous trees, and this clearing, and the stream here, or perhaps this lake; that luxuriant meadow would also look nice in my garden, or a strip of seashore and a ruin of a Gothic cloister would be splendid. And I should like to

have that ancient lime-tree there, and that antique fountain would also do quite well; and how about a herd of stags, or some chamois, or at least this avenue of old poplars; that rock there, this river, that oak grove, or that foaming waterfall, or at least this quiet and green dell——"

If it were possible to make a compact with the devil, who would then gratify every wish, the gardener would sell him his own soul; but for this soul the poor devil would pay damnably dear. "You miserable fellow," he would say at the end, "rather than slave like this, get yourself gone to Paradise—in any case it's the only place for you." And lashing his tail in irritation, till he knocked off the flowers of the feverfew and helenium with it, he would go on his business, and leave the gardener to his immodest and inexhaustible desires.

Understand that I am talking of the real gardener and not of apple-growers and market gardeners. Let the apple-grower beam over his apples and pears, let the market gardener rejoice at the super-human height of his kohlrabi, marrows, and celery; a real gardener feels in his bones that August is already a turning-point. What is in flower hastens to be over; autumn asters and chrysanthemums are still to come, and then good night! But you, shining phlox, the flower of rectory gardens, you, golden groundsel and golden rod, golden rudbeckia and golden harpalium, golden sunflower, you and I, we shall not go under yet, not we! All the year round is spring, and all through life is youth; there is always something which may flower. One only says that it is autumn; we are merely flowering in other ways, we grow beneath the earth, we put forth new shoots; and always there is something to do. Only those who keep their hands in their pockets say that it is getting worse; but who flowers and bears fruit, even in November, knows nothing of the autumn, but of the golden summer; knows nothing of decay, but of germination. Autumnal aster, dear man, the year is so long that you can't see its end.

ON THE CULTIVATORS OF CACTI

WHEN I call them sectarians, it is not because they
cultivate cacti with great enthusiasm, for this
can be put down to passion, eccentricity, or mania.
The gist of sectarianism is not that something is
done passionately, but that something is passionately believed in. There are some cactus-men who
believe in powdered marble, whereas others believe
in brick-dust, and others in charcoal; some approve
of water, while others reject it; there are profound
mysteries in a Real Cactus Soil which no cactus
maniac would betray, even if you broke him on
the wheel. All these sects, observances, rituals,
schools, and lodges, as well as the wild or hermit
cactus maniacs, will swear that only by their Method
alone have they achieved such miraculous results.
Look at this Echinocactus Myriostigma. Did you
ever see anywhere else such an Echinocactus
Myriostigma? So I will tell you, on condition that
you will not tell anyone else, it must not be watered
but sprinkled. That's what it wants.—What!
cries another cactus-man. Who ever heard that
Echinocactus Myriostigma could be sprinkled?
Do you want its crown to catch cold? My dear
sir, if you don't want your Echinocactus to die
straight away of putrefaction you must damp it

only by putting it once a week, with the pot, in soft water, warmed to 23·789° Celsius. Then it will grow like a turnip.—God Amighty! shouts the third cactus-man, look at that murderer! If you damp the pot, sir, it will be covered with Proto-coccus; the soil will get sour, and you will be done for—yes, done for; besides your Echinocactus Myriostigma will rot at the root. If you don't want your soil to turn sour, you must water it every second day with sterilized water, and in such a way that 0·111111 gramme, exactly half a degree warmer than the air, comes on a cubic centimetre. —Then the cactus maniacs begin to shout all together, and attack one another with their fists, teeth, hooves, and claws; but as is the way of this world, the real truth is not brought to light even by these means.

The truth, of course, is that cacti deserve their special cult, if only because they are mysterious. The rose is beautiful, but not mysterious; among the mysterious plants are the lily, gentian, golden fern, the tree of knowledge, ancient trees as a whole, some mushrooms, mandrake, orchids, glacial flowers, poisonous and medicinal herbs, water-lilies, Mesembryanthemum, and cacti. Where the mystery lies I can't say; yet mystery there

must be, if we are to search for it and rever-
ence it. There are cacti just like porcupines,
cucumbers, marrows, candlesticks, jugs, priests'
caps, snakes' nests; they are covered with scales,
teats, tufts of hair, claws, warts, bayonets, yata-
ghans, and stars; they are bulky and lanky, spiked
like a regiment of lancers, sharp like a column
brandishing swords, swollen, stringy, and wrinkled,
pock-marked, bearded, peevish, morose, thorny
like abatis, woven like a basket, looking like
excrescences, animals, and arms; the most masculine
of all plants which were created on the third day,
bearing seed according to their kind. ("Well, I'm
blessed", said the Creator, astonished Himself at
what He had created.) You can love them without
touching them indecently, or kissing them, or
pressing them to your breast; they don't care for
any intimacies and other such frivolities; they are
hard like stone, armed to the teeth, determined not
to surrender; go on, pale face, or I will shoot!
A small collection of cacti looks like a camp of
warlike pigmies. Chop off a head or arm from that
warrior and a new man in arms will grow out of
it, brandishing swords and daggers. Life is war.

But there are mysterious moments when that
obstinate and surly blockhead somehow forgets
himself and falls into dreams; then a flower bursts

out of him, a big, brilliant flower, a sacramental flower in the midst of brandished arms. It is a great favour, and a precious event, which does not happen to everyone. I tell you, a mother's pride is nothing to the boasting and bragging of a cactus-man whose cactus has come into flower.

THE GARDENER'S SEPTEMBER

In its way—from the horticultural point of view—
September is a gratifying and excellent month;
not only because golden rod, autumnal asters, and
Indian chrysanthemums are in flower; not only
because of you, heavy and amazing dahlias; for
know ye, unbelievers, that September is the chosen
month for everything that flowers a second time:
the month of the second flower; the month of the
ripening wine. All these are mysterious advantages
for the month of September, full of deeper mean-
ing; and, above all, it is the month when the earth
opens so that *we can plant* again! Now those things
should go into the ground which must get a hold
before the spring; this affords us gardeners an
opportunity for running again to the nurserymen
to look at their beds and choose treasures for the
coming spring; and besides, it gives me an excuse
to stop in the circuit of the year to pay a tribute
to those worthy men.

The great gardener, or nurseryman, is usually
a teetotaller and a non-smoker; in a word, he is a
very virtuous man; he is not known in history by
prominent crimes, or by warlike or political acts;
his name is immortalized by some new rose or
dahlia, or apple; this fame—usually anonymous,

or hidden behind another name—is sufficient for him. By some trick of Nature he is usually a corpulent and almost enormous man, perhaps to produce a suitable contrast to the slender filigree delicacy of the flowers; or Nature has made him after the

image of Cybele to symbolize his generous paternity. In fact, if such a nurseryman pokes with his finger in the pots, it is almost as if he were giving the breast to his little wards. He scorns the garden architects, who in their turn take the nurserymen for market-gardeners. You should know that

114

nurserymen do not consider cultivation to be a craft, but a science and art; it is almost crushing when they say of a competitor that he is a good business man. One does not go to the nurseryman as to a vendor of collars or hardware, to say what one wants to buy, to pay and then to go away. One goes to the nurseryman to talk, to ask what this is called, and to tell him that that hutchinsia which you bought last year is doing very well; to complain that this year mertensias suffered, and to beg him to show you what novelties he has got. One ought to discuss with him whether Rudolph Göthe or Emma Bedau (these are asters) is better, and argue whether Gentiana Clusii does better in peat or in loam.

After discussing these and many other topics you choose one new alyssum (but, damn, where shall I put it?), one larkspur, in place of the one which you lost through blight, and one pot about which you cannot agree with him as to what it really is; and having spent thus a few hours in an illuminating and gentle amusement you pay him, who is not a business man, about eightpence or tenpence, and that's all. And yet such a real nurseryman likes to have you pester him better than the plutocrats who come stinking in a car and set him to choose sixty kinds of "the best flowers, but they must be first class".

Every nurseryman swears that his soil is thoroughly bad, that he does not manure, or water, or cover in winter; by this apparently he wants to say that his flowers grow so well out of pure affection to him. There is something in it; a man must

have a lucky hand in gardening, or a kind of a higher grace. A real gardener can stick a bit of a leaf in the ground and any plant will grow out of it, while we laymen nurse the seedlings, water them, breathe on them, feed them with horn or baby powder; and finally they droop somehow and

116

shrivel away. I think that there is some magic in it, as in hunting and medicine.

To produce a new species, that is the secret dream of every passionate gardener! Good Lord, if I

only could produce a yellow forget-me-not, or a forget-me-not-blue poppy, or a white gentian!——
What, the blue one is prettier? It does not matter; but a white gentian has not been seen yet. And then, you know, even in flowers the man is a little of a chauvinist; if a Czech rose were to win at a

show against the American "Independence Day" or French "Herriot", we should swell with pride and burst with joy.

I advise you sincerely that if you have in your

garden a bit of a slope, or a small terrace, make a rock garden there. In the first place, such a rock garden is very beautiful when it is grown over with cushions of saxifrage, aubretia, alyssum, wall cress, and other very nice little Alpine flowers; secondly, because making a rock garden is itself a splendid and fascinating exercise. A man who builds a rock garden feels himself to be a Cyclops when he, so to speak, with elemental power, piles stone upon stone, creates hills and dales, transports mountains and erects rocky cliffs. Later, when with aching back he has finished his gigantic masterpiece, he finds that it looks rather different from the romantic mountain which he had in mind; and it seems to be only a heap of rubble and stones. But don't worry; in a year these stones will change into a most beautiful bed, sparkling with tiny flowers, and grown over with nice green cushions; and your pleasure will be great. I tell you, make a rock garden.

We can't deny it any longer; it is autumn. You will recognize it in the flowering of the autumnal chrysanthemums—these autumnal flowers bloom with special vigour and fullness; they don't make much fuss, one flower is like the other, but how many they are! I tell you that this flowering of mature age is more vigorous and passionate than those restless and passing tossings of the young spring. In it there is the sense and consistency of a grown-up man; if you flower, do it thoroughly; and have plenty of honey so that the bees will come. What is a falling leaf to this rich autumnal display? Or don't you see that there is no exhaustion?

119

THE SOIL

WHEN mother in her young days was telling her fortune from cards she always whispered over one pile: "What am I treading on?" Then I could not understand why she was so interested in what she was treading on. Only after very many years did it begin to dawn on me. I discovered that I was treading on the earth.

In fact, one does not care what one is treading on; one rushes somewhere like mad, and at most one notices what beautiful clouds there are, or what a beautiful horizon it is, or how beautifully blue the hills are; but one does not look under one's feet to note and praise the beautiful soil that is there. You must have a garden, though it be no bigger than a pocket-handkerchief; you must have one bed at least to know what you are treading on. Then, dear friend, you will see that not even clouds are so diverse, so beautiful, and terrible as the soil under your feet. You will know the soil as sour, tough, clayey, cold, stony, and rotten; you will recognize the mould puffy like pastry, warm, light, and good like bread, and you will say of this that it is beautiful, just as you say so of women or of clouds. You will feel a strange and sensual pleasure if your stick runs a yard deep

into the puffy and crumbling soil, or if you crush
a clod in your fingers to taste its airy and tepid
warmth.

And if you have no appreciation for this strange
beauty, let fate bestow upon you a couple of rods
of clay—clay like lead, squelching and primeval
clay out of which coldness oozes; which yields
under the spade like chewing-gum, which bakes
in the sun and gets sour in the shade; ill-tempered,
unmalleable, greasy, and sticky like plaster of
Paris, slippery like a snake, and dry like a brick,
impermeable like tin, and heavy like lead. And now
smash it with a pick-axe, cut it with a spade, break
it with a hammer, turn it over and labour, cursing
aloud and lamenting.

Then you will understand the animosity and
callousness of dead and sterile matter which ever
did defend itself, and still does, against becoming
a soil of life; and you will realize what a terrible
fight life must have undergone, inch by inch, to
take root in the soil of the earth, whether that life
be called vegetation or man.

And then you will know that you must give
more to the soil than you take away; you must
make it friable and fertile with lime, and temper it
with warm manure, lighten it with ashes, and
saturate it with air and sunshine. Then the baked

clay disintegrates and crumbles as if it breathed in
silence; it breaks down under the spade with
surprising readiness; it is warm and malleable in
the hand; it is tamed. I tell you, to tame a couple
of rods of soil is a great victory. Now it lies there,
workable, crumbly, and humid; you would like
to take it and rub it all between your thumb and
finger, to assure yourself of your victory; you
think no more of what you will sow in it. Is it not
beautiful enough, this dark and airy soil? Is it not
more beautiful than a bed of pansies or carrots?
You are almost jealous of the vegetation which
will take hold of this noble and humane work
which is called the soil.

And from that time on you will not go over the
earth unconscious of what you are treading on.
You will try with your hand and stick every heap
of clay, and every patch in a field, just as some
other men look at stars, at people, or violets; you
will burst into enthusiasm over the black humus,
fondly rub the smooth woodland leafmould,
balance in your hand the compact sod and weigh
the feathery peat. O Lord! you will say, I should
like to have a wagon of this; and heavens! a cartload of this leafmould would do me good; and
this humus here for putting on the top, and here
a couple of those cow pancakes, and a little bit of

that river sand, and some rings of these rotten wood stumps, and here a bit of sludge from the stream, and sweepings from the road would not be bad either, would they? and still some phosphate and horn shavings, but this beautiful arable soil would also suit me. Great Scott! There are soils as fat as bacon, light as feathers, crumbly like a cake, blond or black, dry or inflated with damp; all these are diverse and noble kinds of beauty; while all that is greasy, cloddy, wet, tough, cold, and sterile is ugly and rotten, unredeemed matter, given to man for a curse; and it is as ugly as the coldness, callousness, and malice of human souls.

THE GARDENER'S OCTOBER

ONE says October; one says Nature lies down to sleep; the gardener knows better, and will tell you that October is as good a month as April. You ought to know that October is the first spring month, the month of underground germination and sprouting, of hidden growth, of swelling buds; scratch a little into the ground and you will find buds ready made, thick as your thumb, fragile shoots and struggling roots—I can't help you, *Spring* is here; go out, gardener, and plant (but be careful that you don't cut with the spade a sprouting narcissus bulb).

Well, then, among all the months October is the month of planting and transplanting. In the early

spring the gardener stands over his bed, from which here and there some spike of buds begins to peep forth, and he says thoughtfully: Here it is a bit bald and empty, I must add something. After some months the gardener stands over the same bed, on which in the meantime six-foot long tails of delphiniums, jungles of feverfew, forests of campanulas, and the devil knows what else, have grown, and he says thoughtfully: Here it is a bit too crowded, I must—er, thin it out, and transplant. —In October the gardener stands over the same bed, out of which here and there a bald stalk, or a withered leaf, sticks; and he says thoughtfully: Here it is a bit bald and empty, I must add something, perhaps six phloxes, or a taller aster. And he goes and does it. The life of a gardener is full of change and active will.

Murmuring with secret satisfaction the gardener finds in October *empty spaces* in his garden. Tut, tut, he says to himself, something must have died here. Let's see, I must plant something in that empty spot; how about golden rod, or perhaps bugwort? I haven't got it in my garden yet; astilbe would look well here; but for autumn Pyrethrum uliginosum would do, though in spring leopard's bane would not be bad here either; well, I shall put a monarda here—either Sunset or Cambridge Scarlet; no doubt a day lily would look very nice here too. After that he wanders home in deep meditation, remembering on the way that morina is a nice little plant, not to mention coreopsis, and even betonica is not so bad; then in haste he orders from some nursery golden rod, bugwort, astilbe,

Pyrethrum uliginosum, leopard's bane, horse mint, day lily, morina, coreopsis, betonica, and still he writes down anchusa and salvia, and then he rages for some days because they do not arrive; at last the postman brings a crate full of them, and then he

throws himself with his spade on that *bald spot*. With the first spit he forces out a mass of roots, on the top of which a whole clump of fat buds is clustered. God Almighty! moans the gardener, I've got trollius here!

Yes, there are maniacs who want to have in

their garden everything that belongs to sixty-eight
genera of Dicotyledons, fifteen genera of Mono-
cotyledons, two genera of Gymnosperms—of the
Cryptogams at least all the Filices, for with Lyco-
pods and Mosses there is trouble. Along with these
there are maniacs, still more absurd, who dedicate
their lives to one species, which, moreover, they
want and must have in every cultivated and named
variety. Thus, for instance, there are Bulb-men
devoted to the culture of tulips, hyacinths, lilies,
chionodoxas, narcissi, tazettas, and other bulbous
marvels; further, Primula- and Auricula-men, who
swear allegiance entirely to primroses, as well as
Anemone-men initiated into the order of wind-
flowers; then Iris- or Flag-men, who would die
of grief if they had not everything that belongs to
the groups Apogon, Pogoniris, Regelia, Onocyclus,
Juno, and Xiphium, not counting the hybrids;
there are Delphinists, cultivating larkspurs, there
are Rose-men or Rosarians, who associate only
with Mrs. Druschki, Mrs. Herriot, Mrs. Caroline
Testout, Mr. Wilhelm Kordes, Mr. Pernet, and
numerous other personalities who are reincarnated
as roses; there are fanatical Phlox-men or Philo-
phloxers, loudly sneering at Chrysanthemum-men,
which courtesy these return in October, when
Chrysanthemum indicum is in flower; there are

melancholy Aster-men, who to all other gratifica-
tions of life prefer the autumnal aster; but of all
the maniacs the wildest (besides, of course, the
Cactus-men) are the Dahlia-men, or Georgians,[1]
who for some new American dahlia will pay a
dizzy sum, perhaps even ten shillings. Of all these
sects only Bulb-men have some kind of historical
tradition, and even their own patron saint, St.
Joseph, who, as is well known, has in his hand
Lilium candidum, although to-day he might have
had Lilium Brownii leucanthum, which is still
whiter. On the other hand, no saint appears with a
phlox or a dahlia, therefore people devoted to the
culture of these flowers are Nonconformists, and
sometimes they even found their own churches.

Why should those cults not have their own
"Lives of the Saints"? Let us imagine, shall we say,
the life of St. Georginus of Dahlia. Georginus was
a virtuous and pious gardener, who after long
prayers and fastings succeeded in raising the first
dahlia. When the heathen Emperor Phloxinian
heard of it, he raged with fury, and sent his bailiffs
to arrest the pious Georgian. "You potato grower!"
the Emperor Phloxinian thundered. "Bow down
to these faded phloxes!" "I will not," said Georgi-

[1] This is a pun on the Czech name for dahlias, which is *jiřina*
or *georgina*.

nus firmly, "because dahlias are dahlias, and a phlox is only a phlox." "Cut him to pieces!" shrieked the cruel Phloxinian; and they cut St. Georginus of Dahlia to pieces, and laid waste his garden, and sprinkled it with green vitriol and

Sctus Georginus ora pro nobis

sulphur; but out of the cut pieces of St. Georginus's body tubers of all the future dahlias sprouted, that is of the peony and anemone dahlias, of the single, cactus and starry dahlias, of Pompon, Mignon, and Tom Thumb dahlias, of Rosette and Collarette dahlias, and of all the hybrids.

Such an autumn is a very fertile time; spring compared with it is a bit fastidious; autumn likes to work on a grander scale. Does it ever happen that a spring violet grows to a height of ten feet, or

that a tulip grows and grows until it overshadows the trees? Am I not right? But you may plant an autumnal aster in spring, and before October a forest ten feet high has shot up, where you dare not enter because you would not find your way out; or you may have put into the ground a root of

131

helianthus or sunflower in April, and now golden flowers wave ironically at you from above, so that you can't reach them with your hand, not even if you stand on tiptoe. Things often get out of proportion in a garden. Therefore in autumn the shifting of flowers is performed; every year the gardener carries his perennials about like a cat her kittens; every year he says with satisfaction: So, now I have it all planted and in order. Next year he sighs with the same satisfaction. A garden is never finished. In that sense it is like the human world and all human undertakings.

ON THE BEAUTIES OF AUTUMN

I COULD write on the riotous colours of the fall, on dismal fogs, on the souls of the dead, and on signs in the sky, on the last asters, and on the red rose which still tries to flower; or on the lights in the evening, on the odour of the cemetery candles, on dry leaves, and other sentimental objects. But I should like to give testimony and praise to another glory of our Czech autumn. It is simply sugar-beet.

No harvest is handled in such masses as sugar-beet. Corn is brought to barns and potatoes into cellars; but sugar-beet is carted into heaps; it aggregates into hills; grows into sugar-beet mountains beside the little country railway-stations. In wagon after wagon white cones are carried in an infinite procession, from morning till night—men with shovels throw the heaps higher and higher, and build them neatly into geometrical pyramids. Every other product of the earth somehow spreads in all directions along narrow paths to all the people's dwellings. Sugar-beet flows in one stream: to the nearest railway-line, or to the nearest sugar factory. It is a wholesale harvest; it is a march *en masse*; it is like a military parade. There are brigades, divisions, and army corps which present themselves for transport. There-fore they are put into military order; geometry, that is the beauty of masses. Sugar-men build their silos like monumental angular constructions; it is a kind of architecture. A heap of potatoes is not a construction; but a heap of sugar-beet is no more a pile, it is an edifice. People from the towns don't like sugar-beet districts very much; but now, in autumn, they possess a kind of dignity of their own. A regular pyramid of sugar-beet is something striking. It is a monument to the fruitful earth.

But allow me to sing the praise of the most humble beauty of autumn. I know that you have no field, and do not cart sugar-beet into big heaps; but did you ever manure a garden? When they bring you a whole wagonload and turn it out, a warm smoking pile, you walk round it, weigh it with your eyes and nose, and say approvingly: "God bless it, it's nice manure."

"Nice," you say, "but a bit light."

"Downright straw", you grumble. "There is very little dung in it."

"Go away, you, who hold your noses, walking in a wide circle round this noble and puffy heap; you don't know what nice manure is." And after the beds have got what they need, one has a slightly mystic feeling of having done some good to the earth.

ON THE BEAUTIES OF AUTUMN

Bare trees, they are not such a desolate sight; they look a bit like besoms or birches, and a bit like scaffolding for building. But if there is one leaf left trembling in the wind on a naked tree, it is like the last flag flying on the battlefield, like a standard which the hand of a dead man is holding on the field of the slain. We have fallen, but we have not surrendered. Our colours are still waving.

And still the chrysanthemums have not given up. They are fragile and airy, only a splash of white or pink foam, chilled like little ladies in dancing-frocks. No sunshine, grey choking fogs, driving sleety rains—is that what you complain of? Never mind. The only thing is to flower. Men complain of bad conditions; chrysanthemums stick to their guns.

Even gods have their seasons. In summer one may be a pantheist, may consider oneself part of Nature, but in autumn one can only take oneself for a human being. Even if we don't cross ourselves we all slowly return to the nativity of man. Every home fire burns to the honour of the household gods. Love of one's home is a rite, similar to the veneration of some celestial godhead.

THE GARDENER'S NOVEMBER

I KNOW that there are many fine jobs; for instance, to write for the papers, to be a Member of Parliament, to sit on a board of directors, or to sign official forms; but however nice and meritorious they may be in these occupations man does not cut such a figure, and has not such a monumental, plastic, and almost statuesque attitude as a *man with a spade*. Ah, when you stand on your bed, leaning with one leg on your spade, wiping the sweat and saying "Ouf," you look just like an allegorical statue; all you need is to be dug up carefully, roots and all, and put on a pedestal with the inscription "*Work triumphant*", or "*Lord of the Earth*", or something like that. I refer to it because just now is the time for it, I mean for digging.

Yes, in November the soil should be turned over and loosened: to lift it with a full spade gives you a feeling as appetizing and gratifying as if you lifted food with a full ladle, with a full spoon. A good soil, like good food, must not be either too fat, or heavy, or cold, or wet, or dry, or greasy, or hard, or gritty, or raw; it ought to be like bread, like gingerbread, like a cake, like leavened dough; it should crumble, but not break into lumps; under the spade it ought to crack, but not

136

HOMO
HORT. EDULIS

to squelch; it must not make slabs, or blocks, or honeycombs, or dumplings; but, when you turn it over with a full spade, it ought to breathe with pleasure and fall into a fine and puffy tilth. That is a tasty and edible soil, cultured and noble, deep and moist, permeable, breathing and soft—in short,

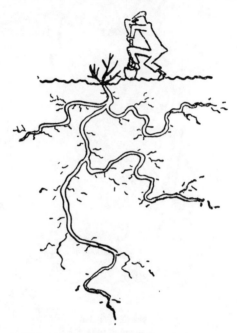

a good soil is like good people, and as is well known there is nothing better in this vale of tears.

You ought to know, you man of the garden, that in these autumnal days you can still *transplant*. First the bush, or tree, is dug and raked round as

138

deeply as possible; then it is lifted from underneath, and then usually the spade snaps in two. There are some people, especially critics and public speakers, who love to talk about roots; they proclaim, for instance, that we ought to return to the roots; or that some evil should be exterminated root and branch, or that we ought to penetrate to the root of some matter. Well, I should like to see how they would set about digging up (roots and all), say, a three-year-old quince. I should like to be a spectator when Dean Inge dives to the root of only such a small bush as Ruscus. I should like to watch how Bernard Shaw uproots, let us say, an oldish poplar. I think that after some toil they would straighten their backs and utter one word. I would bet my boots that that word would be "Damn!" I tried it with cydonia; and I am ready to agree that a job with roots is a heavy job; it is better to leave roots where they are; they know why they want to go so deep; I should say that they don't care for our attention. It is better to leave the roots alone and improve the soil instead.

Yes, improve the soil. A cartload of manure is most beautiful when it is brought on a frosty day, so that it steams like a sacrificial altar. When its fragrance reaches heaven, He who understands all things sniffs and says: "Um, that's some nice manure."—Here, of course, we have an opportunity to talk of the mysterious cycle of life; a horse chews oats, and then he sends them on to

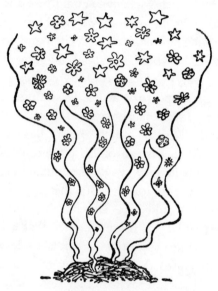

the carnations or roses, which next year will praise God for the gift with such a sweet perfume that is beyond description. This sweet perfume the gardener notices already in the reeking and strawy heap of manure; and he sniffs approvingly, and he carefully spreads this gift of God over the whole garden as if he were spreading marmalade on his child's bread. Here you are, little chum, may you enjoy it! To you, Mrs. Herriot, I shall give a whole pile, because you flowered so finely and richly; you, feverfew, will get this cake to keep you quiet; and with this brown straw I will make a bed for you, you zealous phlox.

Good people, why do you screw up your face? Don't you like my smell?

Yet a little while and we shall do our garden the last service; we will still allow one or two early frosts to come, and then we shall bed it in green brushwood; we shall bend the roses and scrape soil up to their necks, we shall spread resinous spruce branches over the beds, and then good night. Usually one covers up something else with this brushwood, a pocket-knife or a pipe; in spring, when we take the brushwood away, we shall meet with everything again.

But we are going too quickly, we have not stopped flowering yet; still the Michaelmas daisy blinks with its lilac eyes, the primroses and the violets flower as a sign that even November is spring; the Indian chrysanthemum (so called because it is not from India, but from China) does not let any atmospheric or political conditions prevent it, be they ever so bad, from producing all its fragile and immense profusion of flowers, of fox-reddish and glistening white, golden and garnet flowers; still the rose bears its last blooms. Queen of plants, you have been flowering for six months, it is your royal duty.

And then the leaves are flowering: the autumn leaves; yellow, purple, flaming red, orange, paprica scarlet, blood red; and red, orange, black, and dusty blooming berries; and yellow, reddish, and blond wood of the naked branches; and still we have not finished. Even when they will be buried in snow, there will still be the dark-green holly with glowing red berries, and black pines, and little cypresses and yews; there is never an end.

I tell you, there is no death; not even sleep. We only pass from one season to another. We must be patient with life, for it is eternal.

But even you who have no bed of soil of your own can worship Nature in this autumn-time—that is, by planting bulbs of hyacinths and tulips in pots, which during winter will either freeze or open into flower. It is done like this: you buy any bulbs you like, and from the nearest gardener you get a sack of nice compost; then you look for all the old flower-pots in the cellar and in the loft, and put one bulb in each. At last you find that you still have some bulbs, but no flower-pots. You buy more pots, and then you discover that you have no bulbs, but pots and soil left over. After that you buy a few bulbs more, but because again you have not soil enough, you buy a new sack of compost. Then again some soil remains over, which, of course, you don't like to throw away, so you decide to buy some more pots and bulbs. In this way you go on until people at home put a stop to it. Then you fill the windows, tables, wardrobes, larder, cellar, and loft with them, and quietly and confidently you await the coming winter.

PREPARATIONS

Why try to conceal it? Already there are unmistakable signs that Nature is lying down to her winter sleep. Leaf after leaf drops from my birches with a beautiful and sad motion; when they have flowered the plants withdraw again into the earth; after they have grown and blossomed they leave behind only a naked stalk or a moist stump, a crabbed brush or a withered stem; and the soil itself smells sadly of decay. Why try to conceal the fact? It is finished for this year. Chrysanthemum, don't deceive yourself about the fullness of life; little white potentilla, don't confuse this last sunshine with the exuberant brilliance of March. It is of no use to complain, children, the parade is over; lie down gently to your winter sleep.

But no! But no! What do you mean? Don't say that! What kind of a sleep is this? Every year we say that Nature lies down to her winter sleep; but we have not yet looked closely at this sleep; or, to be more precise, we have not looked at it yet from below. You must turn things upside down to know them better; Nature must be turned upside down so that you can look into it; turn her roots up. Good Lord, is this sleep? You call this a rest? It would be better to say that vegetation has ceased to grow upwards, because it has no time for it now; for it has turned its sleeves up and grows downwards, it spits in its hands and digs itself into the ground. Look, this pale thing here in the earth is a mass of new roots; look how far they push; heave-ho! heave-ho! Can't you hear how the earth is cracking under this enraged and collective charge? I beg to announce, general, that the storm troops of roots have won their way into the enemies' ground; the scouts of phloxes came into contact with the advance patrols of the campanulas. All right; let them dig themselves in in the conquered territory; the objectives have been gained.

And these fat, white, and frail things here are new germs and shoots. See how many there are; how bushy you have recently become, faded and withered perennial, how self-confident you are, how overflowing with life! You call this sleep? May the devil take leaves and flowers! Don't be sentimental! Here below, here underground, is the real work, here, here, and here new stems are growing; from here to there, within these November limits, the life of March will spring up; here underground the great programme of spring is laid down. The time to rest has not come yet;

look, here is the plan of the building, here the foundations are dug and the drains are laid; and we shall sap further yet, before the soil hardens in the frost. Let spring build green vaults over the pioneer work of the autumn. We underground forces have done our duty.

A hard and fat bud underground, a swelling on the top of a bulb, a strange outgrowth under the heels of dry foliage, a bomb out of which a spring flower will burst. We say that spring is the time for germination; really the time for germination is autumn. While we only look at Nature it is fairly true to say that autumn is the end of the year; but still more true it is that autumn is the beginning of the year. It is a popular opinion that in autumn leaves fall off, and I really cannot deny it; I assert only that in a certain deeper sense autumn is the time when in fact the leaves bud. Leaves wither because winter begins; but they also wither because spring is already beginning, because new buds are being made, as tiny as percussion caps out of which the spring will crack. It is an optical illusion that trees and bushes are naked in autumn; they are, in fact, sprinkled over with everything that will unpack and unroll in spring. It is only an optical illusion that my flowers die in autumn; for in reality they are born. We say that Nature rests, yet she is working like mad. She has only shut up shop and pulled the shutters down; but behind them she is unpacking new goods, and the shelves are becoming so full that they bend under the load. This is the real spring; what is not done now will not be done in April. The future is not in front of us, for it is here already in the shape of a germ; already it is with us; and what is not with us will not be even in the future. We don't see germs because they are under the earth; we don't know the future because it is within us. Sometimes we seem to smell of decay, encumbered by the faded remains of the past; but if only we could see how many fat and white shoots are pushing forward in the old tilled soil, which is called the present day; how many seeds germinate in secret; how many old plants draw themselves together and concentrate into a living bud, which one day will burst into flowering life—if we could only see that secret swarming of the future within us, we should say that our melancholy and distrust is silly and absurd, and that the best thing of all is to be a living man—that is, a man who grows.

THE GARDENER'S DECEMBER

YES, you are right, everything is now finished. Until now he has hoed, dug, loosened, turned over, manured, and dressed with lime; strewn the soil over with peat, ashes, soot; cut, sown, planted, transplanted, divided, put bulbs in the ground, and taken out tubers for the winter; sprinkled and watered, cut the grass, weeded, covered the plants with brushwood, or raked soil to their necks —all this he did between February and December, and only now, when the garden is buried in snow, does he remember that he has forgotten something: to look at it. For you must know that until now he has had no time to do that. When in summer he ran to look at a flowering gentian he had to stop on the way to weed the grass. When he wanted to enjoy the beauty of delphiniums in bloom he found that he had to give them supports. When asters came into flower he ran to fetch a can to water them. When phlox flowered he pulled out couch-grass; when roses were in bloom he looked where to cut side-branches, or how to destroy rust; when chrysanthemums began to open he ran for a hoe to loosen the soil which had settled round their roots. What do you expect? There was always something to do; how, then, could he put his hands in his pockets and just look to see what things are like?

Now, thank God, everything is finished; perhaps there are still things to be done; there at the back

the soil is like lead, and I rather wanted to transplant this centaurea, but peace be with you; the snow has already fallen. What would you say, gardener, if for the first time you *looked at* your garden?

Well, this black thing here, which is sticking out of the snow, is a withered viscaria; this dry stalk is a blue aquilegia; that tuft of shrivelled leaves is astilbe; and look, that sweep there is Aster ericoides; and here, where there is nothing at all, there is an orange trollius; and this heap of snow here is dianthus, of course it is dianthus. And that stem is perhaps the red yarrow.

Brr, it is cold! Even in winter one can't enjoy one's garden.

Well, then, make a fire in my room; let the garden sleep under its eiderdown of snow. It is good to think of other things as well; the table is full of books which we have not read, let's do that; we have so many other plans and cares, let's make a beginning. But have we covered up everything well with brushwood? Have we wrapped up tritonia? Haven't we forgotten to cover the plumbago? Kalmia ought to be protected by a branch; what if azalea gets frozen? What if the tubers of the Asiatic ranunculus don't come up next year? In that case we shall plant instead . . . wait. . . . Wait a bit, let's look through some catalogues.

So in December the garden is mostly found in a great number of garden catalogues. The gardener himself hibernates under glass in a heated room, buried up to the neck, not in manure or brushwood, but in garden catalogues and circulars, books and pamphlets, in which he reads:

1. That the most valuable, gratifying, and

altogether indispensable plants are those which he has not got in his garden;

2. That all that he has is "rather delicate", and is "inclined to get frozen"; or that he planted side by side one plant "which requires moisture", and another "which must be protected against damp"; that the one which he planted with special care in

the open sunshine requires "full shade", and vice versa;

3. That three hundred and seventy, or more, kinds of plants exist which "deserve better attention", and "ought not to be left out of any garden",

or which are at least "perfectly new and surprising varieties, surpassing by far all previous ones".

Conscious of all that the gardener usually becomes very melancholy in December; first he begins to be frightened that in spring not one of his plants will come up because of frost or fungi,

152

moisture, drought, sunshine, and lack of sunshine; he racks his brains, therefore, how to fill up these terrible gaps.

Secondly, he finds that even if very few die, he will have hardly any of those "most valuable, profusely flowering, entirely new, and unsurpassed" varieties of which he has just read in sixty catalogues; this is indeed an intolerable blank which must be filled up somehow. Then the hibernating gardener ceases entirely to be interested in what he has got in his garden, being fully occupied with what he has not, which of course is far more; he throws himself eagerly upon catalogues, and ticks off what he must order, which, by Jove, must no longer be lacking in his garden. In the first rush he marks off four hundred and ninety perennials which he must order at all costs; after counting them he is a bit subdued, and with a bleeding heart he begins to cross off those which he will give up for this year. This painful elimination must be gone through five times at least, until only about one hundred and twenty "most beautiful, gratifying, indispensable" perennials remain, which —on the wings of an anticipated joy—he immediately orders. "Send them at the beginning of March!"—Lord, if only it were March already! he thinks in feverish impatience.

But God has blinded him; in March he discovers that with the utmost difficulty he can find not more than two or three places in his garden where it is possible to plant anything, and even those are

near the hedge behind the bushes of Japanese quinces.

After he has done this most important, and—as you see—rather hurried winter work, the gardener begins to be desperately bored; because "it will begin in March", he counts the days to March, and because there are too many, he subtracts fifteen days because "sometimes it begins in February". It's no use, he must wait. Then the gardener throws himself on something else, say on a sofa, couch, or settee, and tries to imitate the winter sleep of Nature.

In half an hour he flies up from this horizontal position, inspired by a new idea. Flower-pots! Aren't flowers grown in pots? At once thickets of palms, latanias, dracaenas, and tradescantias, asparagus, clivias, and begonias, in all their tropical beauty, rise before his eyes; and among them, of course, a forced primula, and hyacinth, and cyclamen will flower; in the corridor we shall make an equatorial jungle, hanging tendrils will flow from the stairs, and in the windows we shall put plants which will flower like mad. Then he glances quickly round; no longer does he see the room in which he lives, but a forest of paradise which he will create here, and he runs to the gardener at the corner to bring home an armful of the treasures of vegetation.

When he brings home as much as he can carry he finds:

That when he puts it all together it does not

look at all like an equatorial forest, but rather like a small crockery shop;

That he can't put anything in the windows because—as the silly women at home declare—windows are for ventilation;

That he can't put anything on the stairs because it would make them filthy with mud and splashed with water;

That he can't change the hall into a tropical forest because, in spite of his fervent entreaties

156

and cursings, the women persist in opening the windows to the frosty air.

So he carries his treasures into the cellar, where, at least, as he comforts himself, it does not freeze; and in spring, poking in the warm soil outside, he forgets them completely. But this experience will by no means deter him next December from trying again with new flower-pots to transform his lodging into a winter garden. In it you see the eternal life of Nature.

ONE says that time brings roses; it is true in a way —usually one must wait for roses until June or July; and as for their growth, three years are sufficient for your rose to make quite a nice top. One ought rather to say that time brings oaks; or that time brings birches. I once planted some birches, saying: "Here there will be a grove of birches; and here in this corner a mighty ancient oak will stand." And I also planted a little seedling oak, but two years have passed, and still there is not a mighty ancient oak, nor are those birches yet a centenary birch grove in which fairies would like to dance. Of course, I shall wait some years yet; we gardeners have immense patience. I have a cedar of Lebanon on my lawn almost as big as I am; according to the experts a cedar can grow to a height of three hundred feet and to a width of fifty feet. Well, I should like to see it when it reaches the pre-scribed height and width; it really would be only fair if I lived as long in good health and, so to speak, reaped the reward of my labours. In the meantime it has grown a good ten inches; well—we must wait.

Take, for example, a little grass plant; if you sow the seed well and sparrows don't pick it up, it pricks through in a fortnight, and in six weeks it needs cutting, but it is not an English lawn yet.

I know an excellent recipe for an English lawn—like the recipe for Worcester Sauce—it comes from an "English country gentleman". An American millionaire said to that gentleman: "Sir, I will pay you anything you like if you will reveal to me by what method such a perfect, even, level, fresh, everlasting, in short, such an English lawn as yours is made."—"That's quite simple", said the English squire. "The soil must be well and deeply dug, it must be fertile and porous, not sour or sticky, not heavy or thin; then it must be well levelled so that it is like a table; after that you sow the seed and roll the ground well; then you water it daily, and when the grass has grown you mow it week after week; you collect the cut grass with sweepers and roll the lawn; you must water, sprinkle, wet, and spray it daily; and if you do this for three hundred years you will have as good a lawn as mine."

To this add that each of us gardeners would like and really ought to examine by actual experience all kinds of roses with regard to their buds, flowers, stems, leaves, crowns, and other features; item all the different kinds of tulips, lilies, irises, delphiniums, carnations, campanulas, astilbes, violets, phloxes, chrysanthemums, dahlias, gladioli, paeonies, asters, primulas, anemones, aquilegias, saxifrages, gentians, sunflowers, day lilies, poppies, golden rods, ranunculi, and veronicas; each of which has at least a dozen of the best and most indispensable classes, varieties, and hybrids; to these one ought to add several hundred genera and species which have only from three to a dozen varieties; further, one should pay special attention to the Alpine, water, and bulbous plants, to heathers and ferns and shade-loving plants, to trees and evergreens; if I were to add all this up I should get, at a very mild estimate, eleven hundred years. The gardener wants eleven hundred years to test, learn to know, and appreciate fully all that is his. I can't make it less, unless I discount 5 per cent. that is for you, and perhaps you need not cultivate the whole lot, although it is well worth while; but you must make haste and not waste a single day, if you want to do what is necessary. You ought to finish what you have begun; you owe it to your garden. I shan't give you a recipe, for you must try yourselves and persevere.

We gardeners live somehow for the future; if roses are in flower, we think that next year they will flower better; and in some few years this little spruce will become a tree—if only those few years were behind me! I should like to see what these birches will be like in fifty years. The right, the best is in front of us. Each successive year will add growth and beauty. Thank God that again we shall be one year farther on!